How to Survive
a Sharknado

and Other Unnatural Disasters

How to Survive a Sharknado

and Other Unnatural Disasters

FIGHT BACK WHEN MONSTERS AND
MOTHER NATURE ATTACK

Andrew Shaffer
With Contributions by Fin Shepard and April Wexler

 THREE RIVERS PRESS • NEW YORK

Published in the United States by Three Rivers Press, an imprint of the Crown
Publishing Group, a division of Random House LLC, a Penguin Random House
Company, New York.
www.crownpublishing.com

Library of Congress Cataloging-in-Publication Data is available upon request.

ISBN 978-0-553-41813-2
eBook ISBN 978-0-553-41814-9

PRINTED IN THE UNITED STATES OF AMERICA

Illustrations by Michael Lee
Book design by Chad Tomlinson
Cover design by Richard Yoo
Back cover illustrations by Michael Lee

10 9 8 7 6 5 4 3 2 1

First Edition

Dedicated to the memories of

Baz Hogan,

George McCallister,

and

April's boyfriend

Semper paratus.

Latin for "Always ready."

—OFFICIAL MOTTO OF THE US COAST GUARD,
AND PERSONAL MOTTO OF FIN SHEPARD

DISCLAIMER

THIS BOOK PROVIDES BASIC ADVICE FOR COPING WITH UNNATU-ral disasters and merciless monsters. However, it is not intended as a substitute for emergency-response training or assistance. Following our recommendations does not guarantee your safety. When in doubt, contact your local authorities for guidance. Has a piranhaconda taken up residence in your garden? Officials will be more than happy to assist you. Unless, of course, they're trying to cover up any mention of the creature because they're secretly responsible for setting it loose in the first place. You wouldn't believe how often that happens. Okay, maybe you would.

CONTENTS

FOREWORD

ONE YEAR AGO, I WAS JUST YOUR TYPICAL FORMER SURF CHAM-pion, bar owner, and deadbeat dad. The day my life changed began like any other. After a late breakfast—brunch, really—I slipped my wetsuit on and grabbed my board to catch a few waves before work. On the news, there was talk about Hurricane David driving large numbers of sharks toward Los Angeles. "Alarmists," I thought. Every time it rains in L.A., everyone swears it's the storm of the century.

This time, they were right.

Before anyone realized what was happening, blue skies gave way to dark clouds. Powerful winds slammed the coast. Torrential rain caused flash flooding throughout the city. Worst of all, sharks washed ashore in droves. They were so thick on the Santa Monica Pier that you had to carry a barstool to beat them away. When the storm temporarily let up, the destruction was unfathomable. My humbly named restaurant, Fin, was reduced to wet kindling.

But the day wasn't over. Not by a long shot. With my ex-wife and children in the storm's path, I couldn't stand around waiting for authorities to do something. I had to take charge. Thankfully, I'd been preparing my whole life for that moment.

Semper paratus.

That's not just my motto. It's my nature. "Always ready." When the storm spawned three deadly sharknados, I was ready. The fact that no one had ever seen a tornado pick up sharks before was irrelevant. It didn't matter if they were filled with bears from the zoo or tigers from Siegfried and Roy's backyard. *Semper paratus* means being ready for anything.

Every time I turn on the TV there's a new threat. Polar vortices. Stonados. Boaricanes. It's not the world I grew up in, but it's the one I live in. It's the one my children live in. They may not carry rappelling gear in their cars like their old man, but they're prepared for whatever Mother Nature has planned. They have to be.

Too many limbs have been lost. Too many lives wasted. And all because people weren't ready. Just like on that horrible day not so long ago, I realized it was time for me to step up. So I sat down with the author of this book and shared my wisdom. My ex-wife, April Wexler, did the same. Everything I know about preparation and survival, everything she's learned along the way—it's all here. Other survivors graciously shared their stories too.

While average citizens like you and me can't prevent unnatural disasters, we can prepare for them. Take a Red Cross–sponsored first-aid class through work. Create a disaster kit in an afternoon with just a few simple items. Know your family's whereabouts at all times. Like, if you know your son is in Van Nuys at flight school, you might want to mention this to your ex-husband who still thinks he's in Florida. That might be helpful information, April.

You don't need to barricade yourself in a log cabin in the middle of nowhere. You don't need a basement full of high-tech weapons, especially when a chainsaw will suffice. What matters most is what's inside your head.

My family and I are ready. Are you? Read this book and count yourself amongst our ranks.

—Finley "Fin" Shepard
Los Angeles, CA
June 2014

INTRODUCTION

I N THE SCIENCE FICTION CLASSIC *THE HITCHHIKER'S GUIDE to the Galaxy,* Douglas Adams joked that Earth is "mostly harmless."

A lot has changed since he wrote that back in the seventies. We've seen sharknados demolish Los Angeles. We've seen meteorites reverse the Earth's polarity. We've seen an eighty-yard mega python swallow one of the Monkees.

Mostly harmless? It's time we upgraded the planet to "mostly harmful."

Mother Nature is angry. Can you blame her? We treat the planet like a rental car with full coverage. Look at our track record over just the past decade. New drilling techniques have exposed hidden dangers below the Earth's surface. Genetic engineers have meddled with the building blocks of life itself, producing terrifying creatures. Don't just blame big business and mad scientists, though. From well-meaning preservationists to bumbling college students on holiday, we're all to blame for Mother Nature's tantrums.

While politicians waste time debating the dangers of fracking and environmentalists wring their hands over our planet's rapid deforestation, we're left with one seriously pissed-off planet.

That's where this book comes in. *How to Survive a Sharknado and Other Unnatural Disasters* provides you with the knowledge necessary to survive dozens of unnatural threats. Whether you're standing face-to-face with a Mongolian death worm or stuck outdoors during a bataclysm, we have you covered.

"But," you say, "I don't need this book. I've seen monster movies. The people who get killed are usually asking for it. All they do is stand there, screaming at the top of their lungs and flailing their arms like those inflatable windsocks at car dealerships."

Put yourself in their shoes. What if you suddenly saw a two-ton great white shark barreling through the air toward your face? Such a sight defies all logic. "That's fake," you mumble. Your brain shorts out. Your legs won't move. Without this book, the best you can hope for is to be killed in a dry pair of underwear.

No matter what we do, it's too late to stop unnatural disasters and monsters. All we can do is survive them.

STUDY — AVOID — SURVIVE

FOR EACH ENTRY, YOU'LL GET A SHORT DESCRIPTION AND VITALS upfront. We follow April Wexler's trademark SAS (Study, Avoid, Survive) methodology. Don't confuse it with Lofty Wiseman's *SAS Survival Guide*—even the vaunted Special Air Service might not be ready for the dangers Mother Nature presents nowadays.

- **Study** the documented incidents.
- **Avoid** the common pitfalls that can put you in harm's way. And when you can't avoid the disaster or monster through preparation . . .

A NOTE ON THE USUAL SUSPECTS

We assume you already know how to defend yourself against commonplace disasters. If you need a refresher on what to do when a tornado siren goes off, the Red Cross has you covered. What about supernatural threats? Frankly, zombies, vampires, and werewolves are now as prevalent as the common cold. We all know about stakes and silver bullets, right? If only fighting Mother Nature were so simple.

• **Survive** by using tips from Fin Shepard as well as others who faced the threats and lived to tell their stories.

HOW THE RATINGS WORK

HOW LIKELY ARE YOU TO ENCOUNTER A SHARKNADO? HOW WIDE-spread will casualties be? And just how badly will your mind be blown? Use the guides below to quickly visualize the magnitude of the threats you'll be reading about.

Threat to Humanity Scale

    💀 = Minimal casualties and damage.

    💀💀 = Serious casualties and damage.

    💀💀💀 = Major casualties and damage on a local scale.

    💀💀💀💀 = Major casualties and damage on a global scale.

💀💀💀💀💀 = Extinction Level Event.

Risk of Encounter Scale

    🌀 = Negligible. No conclusive evidence.

    🌀🌀 = Low. At least one verified sighting, but no indication of how widespread it is.

    🌀🌀🌀 = Moderate. Multiple reports, or repeats expected.

    🌀🌀🌀🌀 = High. Frequent occurrences.

🌀🌀🌀🌀🌀 = Extreme. Under the proper conditions, you will encounter these threats.

Fin Shepard's WTF (Wow, That's Freaky) Factor

    ⚠ = Gnarly. Cool. Righteous.

    ⚠⚠ = Radical. Excellent. Primo.

    ⚠⚠⚠ = Bodacious. Incredible.

    ⚠⚠⚠⚠ = Heavy. Epic.

⚠⚠⚠⚠⚠ = Far Out. Beyond human comprehension.

PART ONE
UNNATURAL DISASTERS

Fighting Mother Nature

ANTDEMIC

ANTDEMIC

VITALS

ALSO KNOWN AS: Insectfluenza
FIRST OBSERVED: Indonesia (2013) • **EST. MAX. SPEED:** 20 mph •
HIGH-RISK GROUPS: Birdwatchers, First Responders • **LOOK OUT
FOR IT IN:** Tropical Areas • **THREAT TO HUMANITY:** 💀💀💀💀 •
RISK OF ENCOUNTER: 🍃🍃🍃 • **FIN'S WTF FACTOR:** ⚠️⚠️

N ANTDEMIC OCCURS WHEN A DEADLY FLU VIRUS is spread to humans by infected mega fire ants. These six-inch winged insects are aggressive and highly contagious, and their bites are excruciating. Even if you survive an attack, your time is limited. Within hours of being bitten, the flu virus reduces you to a violent zombie. Death is the only cure.

STUDY ▪▪▪ THE FIRST ANTDEMIC began in 2013 with a series of mega fire ant attacks on a remote chain of Indonesian islands. As the body count climbed, scientists descended upon the region. Among them was University of Indonesia researcher Eva Sims, who linked the attacks to a deadly flu outbreak also occurring on the islands.

"No one had connected the influenza to the mega fire ants," she says. "But that's exactly what was happening. The ants contracted the virus from attacking infected birds, then passed the virus to humans—who started attacking each other. It was chaos."

Unfortunately, Sims couldn't convince a skeptical World Health Organization (WHO) of the threat. "They told me to stop watching so many zombie movies," she says. If the WHO wouldn't do anything, Sims would. There was still time.

"The virus was not spreading from person to person. If it made that leap, the antdemic could spread worldwide," she says. Her theory was simple: Eliminate the mega fire ants, eliminate the virus. Sims found their breeding ground—a towering mound hidden deep in the jungle—and wiped the ant colony out with the most effective insecticide available: dynamite.

AVOID ▪ ▪ ▪ THE CENTERS FOR Disease Control (CDC) suggests you take the following actions to protect yourself from the next antdemic.

- **Get a flu shot.** This will defend you against the three most common viruses circulating in any given year. Will it protect you during an antdemic? Depends on what flu strain the ants are spreading. Get your annual shot regardless. Not getting vaccinated is like leaving your front door unlocked—you're just inviting trouble. Unless you live in Canada, where no one locks their doors and everyone has hardy immune systems.
- **Avoid contact with anyone exhibiting flu symptoms.** While the last antdemic did not spread from person to person, the next might. Even if it doesn't, people infected with an antdemic

Antdemic Flu Symptoms

- Red, swollen marks where a mega fire ant's pincers penetrated your skin
- Runny nose, usually with blood
- Coughing up blood
- Sore throat (from coughing up blood)

- Fever, body aches, and chills
- Headache, fading as you turn into a zombie
- Unusual aggressive behavior, i.e., chasing and trying to bite strangers

flu strain are kind of a pain to deal with (see the "Antdemic Flu Symptoms" above).

- **Wash your hands frequently with soap and water to kill germs.** Avoid touching your eyes, nose, and mouth. Don't let anyone else touch those areas either. What kind of weirdo would want to touch someone else's eyeball, anyway?

SURVIVE ▪▪▪ ACCORDING TO SIMS, you can't fight back against mega fire ants in any meaningful way. If you're attacked outside, here's what she suggests doing.

- **Dive underwater.** Mega fire ants can fly, but they're poor swimmers. They drown quickly, especially in saltwater and chlorinated pools.
- **If you've been bitten, see a doctor for an antiviral drug.** Unless you receive treatment within two hours, you will turn into a zombie. If there's a full-scale outbreak, the doctor's office may be closed. Postapocalypse rules apply. Join the angry, infected mob ransacking the local pharmacy for antiviral drugs.

ARACHNOQUAKE

ARACHNOQUAKE

VITALS

ALSO KNOWN AS: Spiders of Unusual Size
FIRST OBSERVED: New Orleans, Louisiana (2012) •
EST. MAX. SPEED: 6 mph • **HIGH-RISK GROUPS:**
Former Child Stars, Mardi Gras Revelers • **LOOK OUT FOR
IT IN:** Warm Climates • **THREAT TO HUMANITY:** 💀💀 • **RISK OF
ENCOUNTER:** ⚡⚡ • **FIN'S WTF FACTOR:** ⚠️⚠️⚠️

URVIVE THE FIRST TREMOR OF AN ARACHNO-
quake, and aftershocks are the least of your worries.
The real danger emerges hours later, when subter-
ranean spiders crawl to the surface. These albino
arachnids measure up to thirty inches from skin-
piercing fangs to spinneret and possess the terrifying ability to shoot
six-foot streams of flame. Don't worry, though—they use that as a
last resort. An arachnoquake spider is much more likely to spit paralyzing venom in your face and plunge its mandible claws into your
abdomen, draining your insides. It may spare you for the purpose

of laying eggs under your skin. This will prolong your agony several hours, until the newborns hatch and feast on your paralyzed body.

STUDY ■ ■ ■ WHEN THE 4.5 earthquake hit New Orleans in 2012, officials feared the worst. The epicenter was just twelve miles from the French Quarter—a direct hit to a community still on the rebound from Hurricane Katrina. While structural damage was moderate, the city thankfully suffered no casualties.

It was a short-lived miracle. Thousands of giant spiders soon emerged from fissures in the Crescent City streets, setting their fangs into the unprepared populace.

Although the situation appeared dire, scientists soon discovered the spiders' key weakness. Arachnoquake drones require instructions sent telepathically from their queen to perform even basic tasks such as breathing. Kill her, and the rest die.

Destroying the queen was no small task. The enormous monster was as large as a two-story house. Non-nuclear military weapons had no effect on her. Fortunately, a brave (or foolish) civilian found a way to use the queen's own offensive arsenal against her. Tour guide Paul Grace donned a divesuit and entered the spider's mouth. Once inside, he located the gas tank that fueled her fiery breath. He hooked a copper cable to her tank, slipped out of the spider, and sparked the cable. The queen exploded from the inside out, spraying guts on the buildings surrounding her nest. On cue, the drones fell dead.

"It was like using a burning rag to ignite a car's gas tank," Grace says. "Not that I've ever, uh, done that. How long is the statute of limitations in Louisiana?"

While scientists believe exploratory drilling in the Gulf triggered the arachnoquake, politicians have been reticent to halt exploration or issue moratoriums on new permits. The real question isn't whether more spiders are still living deep below the Earth's surface.

Since they laid eggs aboveground, who's to say a new queen didn't hatch? Come to think of it, she could be amassing her own colony up here right now.

AVOID ▪ ▪ ▪ YOUR SURVIVAL HINGES upon how well you can avoid the spiders' paralyzing venom. Side effects include trouble breathing, muscle rigidity, and blurred vision—if you live that long, of course. Therefore, your life depends on what you wear.

- **Avoid fibers that burn easily.** This includes cotton, linen, rayon, and any blends containing those fibers. Also, ditch the vinyl hot pants—they're liable to melt and stick to your skin when exposed to an open flame.

How to Escape from a Spiderweb

While all arachnoquake spiders are capable of spinning webs, only the queen's web is large enough to trap a human being. So what should you do if you're stuck in her web?

1. Even if you can't see the queen, don't struggle. She may be nearby monitoring her web with a signal line, waiting for good vibrations. The more you move, Marky Mark, the more likely you are to attract her attention.
2. If you have a knife or other sharp weapon, cut yourself free. The first strand to snap will alert the queen to your presence, so work fast. Chop chop!
3. When making your dramatic exit, crawl along one of the web strands that extend outward from the center. Avoid the webbing that runs in concentric circles, as it's the stickiest.
4. Once you've escaped, say something snarky to the queen, like "Sorry I couldn't stick around."

- **Layer your clothing.** Don't worry about trying to match colors, because by the end of the day you'll be covered in spider guts. Tuck your shirtsleeves into your gloves and your pants into your socks. You can't pull this off without looking like a dork. That's okay. Body bags look even dorkier.
- **Wear a gas mask.** Tom Ford and Marc Jacobs had stunning gas masks in their spring 2014 collection. No high-end clothing stores in your area? Try your local Army Surplus.

WEIRD SCIENCE

Arachnoquake spiders live in a colony. While this isn't unique, it is rare. Out of close to 40,000 species of spider, less than two dozen exhibit social behavior. Forget dinner and a movie—most spiders don't socialize outside of mating.

SURVIVE ■ ■ ■ SINCE BUILDINGS WILL likely be compromised due to tremors, you may not be able to find a safe place to hide from the spiders. Be prepared to go on the offensive.

- **Fight the drones.** Despite their thick exoskeletons, arachnoquake spiders are no match for firearms. Shotguns are preferred. Buckshot will tear right through these suckers.

WARNING: *Some arachnoquake spiders may be small enough to smash under the heel of your boot. Doing so would be the equivalent of stepping on a land mine, as their gas tanks are highly explosive.*

- **Fight the queen.** Unlike the drones, this arachnid's exoskeleton is thick enough to protect it from heavy artillery, including grenades. Your best bet is to follow Grace's example and use the queen's gas tank against her. "If you can figure out a less messy way to do that than jumping into her mouth, be my guest," he says.

- **Even after you kill the queen and the drones drop dead, you're not in the clear.** Following an arachnoquake, look out for downed power lines, ruptured gas lines, and (most important) flammable spider corpses. Report all hazards to either utility companies or animal control as appropriate.

BATACLYSM

BATACLYSM

VITALS

ALSO KNOWN AS: Batastrophe
FIRST OBSERVED: Austin, Texas (2011) • **EST. MAX. SPEED:**
25 mph • **HIGH-RISK GROUPS:** Alt-country Musicians, Internet
Celebrities • **LOOK OUT FOR IT IN:** Anywhere • **THREAT TO
HUMANITY:** 💀💀💀 • **RISK OF ENCOUNTER:** ⚡⚡⚡ •
FIN'S WTF FACTOR: ⚠️⚠️

URING A BATACLYSM, IRRADIATED VAMPIRE BATS
are flushed from underground caves by seismic activity. Disoriented from the quake, these oversized
mutants attack anything that moves. They have
wingspans of more than four feet, with grotesque
bodies to match. Their ability to navigate and locate prey in total
darkness makes them difficult to escape from. Once they've found
you, they'll sink their teeth into you and drain your blood (they're
called "vampire bats" for a reason). Even brief contact leads to radiation sickness, especially in children and the elderly.

STUDY ▪ ▪ ▪ SOMETIME IN THE 1970s or 1980s, nuclear waste buried in the outskirts of Austin began leaking out of faulty tanks. While the water supply miraculously avoided exposure, the toxic material seeped into underground caves used by vampire bats. The bats mutated, growing large and hideous.

"We're still trying to discover how they went undetected for so long," says Quentin Rodriguez, a bat researcher with the University of Texas. "These things are big. They walk upright while on the ground. To farmers who caught them feeding on livestock, they probably looked like bloodsucking chupacabra."

When a rare earthquake hit South Texas in March 2011, the mutant bats flooded the streets of Austin. Thousands of people died in the initial onslaught. More perished days and months later because of radiation poisoning.

Rodriguez used a sonic beacon to lure the bats to the newly built Austindome. While the bats slept in the football stadium's rafters during the day, the Texas National Guard demolished the $400 million structure. "The collapse crushed the bats," Rodriguez says. "It also crushed the Texas Longhorns season-ticket holders' new luxury seats. Not a day goes by that I don't get an e-mail about that."

AVOID ▪ ▪ ▪ THIS WASN'T A one-time event, warns Rodriguez. Radioactive waste is buried around the world. Bats live on every continent except Antarctica. That means another bataclysm is just an earthquake away.

- **Wear night-vision goggles.** Bats are nocturnal. Thanks to their use of ultrasonic calls—a technique called echolocation—they can "see" you at night. With a pair of night-vision goggles, you can even the score. Put them on every time the sun goes down. Never be surprised by a bat or burglar again.
- **Shave your head.** Bats are notorious for getting tangled up in

CREEPY FOLKLORE

There's an urban legend that says if a bat flies over the head of a child, it's bad luck and the child stops growing. As strange as it sounds, there is a little truth to this story—at least when it comes to bataclysm bats. If one of them flies close enough to a child, he or she may contract radiation poisoning. While they do stop growing, they also develop special mutant powers. Kids *love* mutant powers.

human hair. If a mutant vampire bat gets stuck in your thick mane, you're almost certainly a goner. Don't risk it. As Patrick Stewart has scientifically proven, bald is sexy.

SURVIVE ▪ ▪ ▪ ONCE YOU RECEIVE word that a bataclysm is happening, seek shelter. If you have important business to conduct that simply can't wait—a Starbucks run, for instance—follow these tips to navigate the bat-infested wastelands outside your front door.

- **Deploy an acoustic jammer at night.** Acoustic jammers interfere with bats' use of echolocation. For an everyday fix try blasting some Barry Manilow from a portable speaker. "For some unknown reason, his voice is on the same wavelength as the echolocation signals of mutant vampire bats," Rodriguez says.

NOTE: *Remember, however, that bats are not blind. Echolocation simply lets them "see" in the dark. If a bat is heading straight for you during the daylight, not even the dulcet tones of Mr. Manilow will slow it down.*

- **Choose your weapons wisely.** There are too many bats in the air during a bataclysm for single-bullet firearms or throwing stars to be of any use. Pick up a weapon that can take out multiple bats at a time, like a shotgun, flamethrower, or reinforced tennis racket.

- **Watch your step.** Be alert for guano. It's not just a pain to scrape off—it's also radioactive.

BEECLIPSE

BEECLIPSE

VITALS

ALSO KNOWN AS: Beeruption
FIRST OBSERVED: Mount St. Helens, Washington (2013) • **EST. MAX. SPEED:** 20 mph • **HIGH-RISK GROUPS:** Lumberjacks, Grunge Musicians, Seahawks • **LOOK OUT FOR IT IN:** Areas Near Volcanoes • **THREAT TO HUMANITY:** 💀💀💀 • **RISK OF ENCOUNTER:** 🌀🌀🌀 • **FIN'S WTF FACTOR:** ⚠️⚠️⚠️

HEN VOLCANOES ERUPT, THEY TYPICALLY release hot gas, debris, and lava. During a beeclipse, however, volcanoes launch something quite different into the air: billions of gigantic honeybees. The bees are the size of fists, with exoskeletons as tough as steel. They crowd the sky, blocking the sun. Don't stare directly into a beeclipse. Not only will you go blind ... you'll go dead. A single sting is enough to kill you unless the stinger is immediately removed. They move in swarms, meaning you'll probably be stung multiple times, decreasing your chances of survival.

STUDY ▪ ▪ ▪ SINCE 2006, WORKER honeybees have been disappearing in record numbers from beehives throughout North America and Europe. Scientists have blamed "colony collapse disorder" on everything from genetically modified foods to cell phone radiation. No one could have guessed the real reason: mass migration to volcanoes.

"Over the years, increasing pesticide use throughout the US drove billions of honeybees to Mount St. Helens," says Violet Steele, a beekeeper who lived near Washington's notoriously active volcano. "The bees found protection there. They turned it into a gigantic beehive."

When a major eruption of hot gas occurred in 2013, so many bees were thrown into the air that they appeared to be a volcanic plume of ash. With the sun blocked out, Steele feared she was reliving the 1980 disaster. It turned out to be worse. By the time anyone deduced the true danger of the darkness, it was too late. The bees swarmed tourists and residents.

Steele knew that honeybees, like other insects, are coldblooded. In order to survive cool temperatures, they huddle together in hives. Steele collaborated with Federal Science Foundation researchers to seed the upper atmosphere with carbon dioxide, causing a sudden cold front. The bees dropped dead, restoring sunlight to Washington. Well, some sunlight at least.

WEIRD DISCOVERY

An ordinary hive produces about a hundred pounds of honey every year. So how much would a hive the size of Mount St. Helens yield? Following the beeclipse, geologists discovered several thousand tons of honey below the surface of the volcano—but don't get too excited, Pooh Bear. Harvesting it is a dangerous proposition. Mount St. Helens is still an active volcano, geologists warn. Any attempt to collect the honey could trigger a massive eruption.

How to Treat a Beeclipse Sting

1. Pluck the stinger out with your thumb and forefinger. The quicker you do this, the better. The venom sets in completely within about three seconds.
2. Wash the area as soon as possible, preferably with hydrogen peroxide or another disinfectant.
3. Swelling will occur within minutes. Apply an ice compress or bag of frozen peas. You were never going to eat them anyway.
4. Take an oral antihistamine containing diphenhydramine (Benadryl) or chlorpheniramine (Chlor-Trimeton). If the venom has had time to set in, you'll need something a little stronger — like an automated external defibrillator (AED).

AVOID ▪ ▪ ▪ NO ONE IS certain where the missing European honeybees are congregating. Another beeclipse seems inevitable. While bees shot out of volcanoes are understandably aggressive, you can still take steps to prevent attacks, says Steele.

- **Don't dress like a flower.** This means no brightly colored clothing, and especially no floral prints. Keep your Hawaiian shirts in the closet.
- **Don't wear perfume or cologne.** Bees love flowery scents. They're the only ones who find your Britney Spears perfume irresistible anyway.
- **Forget bee repellents.** While there are several "natural, herbal" repellents on the market, none are even remotely effective during a beeclipse. Heck, most aren't effective against regular bees.
- **Skip Valentine's Day.** A dozen red roses is a sweet, romantic gesture . . . until a tiny death squad of killer bees swarms your beloved.

SURVIVE ▪ ▪ ▪ DON'T TRY TO swat bees away. This just annoys them further. Use your energy to get to safety as quickly as possible.

- **Choose your shelter wisely.** Massive bee swarms can break through glass. The safest place is an indoor room without windows. Panic rooms and fallout shelters are preferred. Avoid vehicles altogether, except as a last resort.

NOTE: *Walk-in coolers provide an extra layer of security, as bees cannot survive freezing temperatures. Unfortunately, neither can most people. If you put on mittens and a scarf when your apartment temperature dips below 70, don't attempt to hide out in a meat locker.*

- **Secure your room.** A locked door doesn't necessarily mean you're safe. Insects have a knack for sneaking indoors. Take advice from incense-burning teenagers everywhere: Close all vents and put a towel under the door.

Honeybees: Fact or Fiction?

Male honeybees are more dangerous than females.
Fiction. The men ("drones") are harmless. Only female honeybees ("workers") can sting. Since you won't have a chance to determine a bee's gender when it's attacking you, err on the side of caution. Treat all bees as stinging threats.

The queen bee is the leader of the pack.
Fact. There's only one per colony. The queen lays two thousand or more eggs per day. That's one big royal family.

Male honeybees do all the work.
Fiction. The women do the bulk of the work, including hive construction, nursing, and pollen gathering.

Female honeybees don't want no scrubs.
Fact. In the fall, the drones are kicked out of the hive to die in the cold. Since they didn't help build it, they can't take refuge there in the winter.

BOARICANE

BOARICANE

VITALS

ALSO KNOWN AS: Razorback Typhoon
FIRST OBSERVED: Rio de Janeiro, Brazil (2011) •
EST. MAX. SPEED: 40 mph (Cyboars), 200 mph (Swirling Winds) •
HIGH-RISK GROUPS: People Who Are Easily Boared, People Who
Just Groaned at That Pun • **LOOK OUT FOR IT IN:** Coastal Regions
• **THREAT TO HUMANITY:** 🐷🐷🐷 • **RISK OF ENCOUNTER:**
🌀🌀🌀 • **FIN'S WTF FACTOR:** ⚠️⚠️⚠️⚠️

URRICANES ARE CALLED "TRIPLE THREATS" BE-
cause of their strong winds, high waves, and tor-
rential rainfall. Throw in hundreds of robotically
enhanced wild boars, and a hurricane bumps up to
a full-alarm boaricane. Double the size of regular
feral hogs, "cyboars" have hydraulic-powered metal skeletons underneath their flesh and blood. Male cyboars sport stainless-steel
tusks sharp as machetes. To power their robotics, they need to eat
constantly, and often hunt in packs. The cyboars' heavy, squat bodies

allow them to maneuver with ease during hurricanes. When strong winds knock you off balance, cyboars descend in a feeding frenzy.

STUDY ▪ ▪ ▪ CYBOARS WERE ORIGINALLY designed by an American weapons contractor. However, they fell into unsafe hands when a Brazilian drug cartel purchased an assortment of cyboars, which they planned to use to intimidate enemies, on the black market.

Shortly thereafter, a rare southern Atlantic hurricane hit the coast, destroying the cartel's stockade. As the storm raged on, the insatiable cyboars turned on their captors and invaded Rio de Janeiro.

At first, world-class *churrascaria* chef Nicolas Sandoval watched helplessly as the boaricane devastated the city. "My wife said they were finally turning the tables on us. She's a vegetarian. She always hated that I owned a restaurant that served nothing but meat."

Her comment got him thinking. "Those damned dirty pigs were eating the people of my city," he says. "If I didn't step up, who would? No one in Rio de Janeiro had as much experience grilling hogs as me. No one."

Once the wind died down, Sandoval and his waiters strapped on flamethrowers. Weapons in hand, the crew braved the weather to hunt and kill the cyboars.

"I prefer my meat rare," Sandoval says. "But that day, I set my flamethrower to well-done."

AVOID ▪ ▪ ▪ WHENEVER THERE'S A hurricane brewing, there's always the potential for it to be upgraded to a boaricane. Stay vigilant. Watch twenty-four-hour news channels twenty-four hours a day. Never miss a minute of coverage. You'll be among the first to know about potential boaricanes. Twenty-four-hour news channels feed on disasters like a firenado feeds on dry timber.

CUDDLY KILLING MACHINES

We won't lie: as long as you can ignore the glowing red eyes and metal tusks, cyboar piglets are cute. Don't be fooled. These little piggies are just as aggressive as their elders. Remember, they're part robot. As we all know, robots are cold-blooded killers. It doesn't matter how much they remind you of Honey Boo-Boo's teacup pig — treat cyboar piglets with the same fear and respect you would show full-grown cyboars. And by that we mean kill the freaks.

SURVIVE ▦▦▦ DURING A BOARICANE, hunker down in your home unless authorities tell you to evacuate. Stay inside. Draw the shades. Wait out the storm. And if a cyboar breaks through your front door, put it down with an electromagnetic pulse weapon (see **ROBOCROC**). Of course, that's not always possible. What if you're hiking in the jungle and a boaricane hits?

- **Take a tip from T-Pain—get low.** If you can't reach shelter, you'll need to protect yourself from flying debris. Get low to the ground. Curl into a ball. If a flash flood washes you away, you'll roll to safety like a human tumbleweed.

- **Climb a tree.** Wait until the storm has died down to try this gambit. You don't want to scale a tree only to be knocked out by a gale-force wind. Cyboars can't climb trees. You can (or at least you could in middle school).

- **Disrespect your elders.** The leader of a cyboar pack is typically a matriarchal sow—a grandmother. If you're surrounded, try to pick her out. She'll be the one hanging toward the back of the group, grunting orders. Stun or wound her with a weapon, and she may order the pack to retreat. Then again, her grandkids may try to teach you a lesson.

DINONAMI

DINONAMI

F YOU'RE IN THE LUCRATIVE DINOSAUR-CLONING BUSINESS, you'd be hard-pressed to find a better breeding ground for your experiments than an isolated tropical island. Unfortunately, megatsunamis—fast-moving waves up to a kilometer high— happen in the same waters with frightening regularity these days. A dinonami occurs when a megatsunami wipes out a dinosaur island and washes the creatures onto the mainland. While large triceratops or tyrannosauruses are rarely caught up in waves, three-foot-tall velociraptors are frequently swept ashore. Once on land, velociraptors can deftly navigate the floodwaters thanks to their feathered arms and sleek bodies. When they've cornered you, they'll tear your stomach open with the three-inch claws on their hind legs and wait for you to bleed to death before feeding.

STUDY ■ ■ ■ IN 2012, A meteorite impact in the Pacific Ocean triggered a megatsunami off the coast of Japan. The spectacular wave wiped out everything in its path, including a remote island teeming with cloned velociraptors. Authorities believe a rogue nation was breeding the dinosaurs as weapons of war. Either that, or else a slightly unhinged businessman was attempting to create his own Triassic Safari theme park.

The megatsunami continued past the island, finally slamming into the Japanese coast. Thousands of buildings collapsed. As survivors attempted to navigate the flooded streets to safety, they found out they weren't alone. The megatsunami had swept hundreds of velociraptors ashore. Raptor attacks doubled the disaster's death toll.

Paleontologist Yamashita Hayato proposed fighting the dinosaurs with biological warfare. "Since velociraptors are ancestors of modern birds, they share some of the same DNA," he says. "I advised the government to strategically deploy an avian flu strain—one that only affected birds, not humans."

The results were swift and brutal. Within hours, the velociraptors succumbed to the virus. Floodwaters washed their carcasses back out to sea, erasing the second dinosaur age as quickly as it had begun.

STRANGE COINCIDENCE

Dinosaurs were wiped out 65 million years ago by a comet impact. Another rock from space—this time, a meteorite—caused the 2012 dinonami. While no one is suggesting the unnatural disasters are related, no one is suggesting they *aren't* related.

AVOID ▪▪▪ MOST OF THE Earth's population lives in coastal regions prone to dinonamis. Unless you're willing to move fifty miles or more inland, you should wake up every day expecting one.

- **Prepare for a quick exit.** Authorities issue emergency warnings before megatsunamis make landfall. Having a preplanned evacuation route will save you valuable time as the wave moves toward the coast. The farther inland you are—and the higher up you are—the better your chance of surviving the wave. Dinosaurs don't have any trouble running up hills, though, so you're not out of the water yet, so to speak.

- **Always wear a life jacket.** Every time you leave the house. You may get a few stares when you're riding the subway, but *semper paratus* requires sacrifices.

SURVIVE ▪▪▪ YOU WON'T REALIZE a megatsunami is carrying dinosaurs until it's too late. Not that it will make much difference— megatsunamis are deadly enough on their own. Thankfully, the following tips apply to either situation.

- **Put down the surf board.** "The prospect of hanging ten on a

CRAZY CONSPIRACY

Researcher Eva Sims believes the Japanese dinonami is linked to another unnatural disaster—2013's Indonesian antdemic (see **ANTDEMIC**). "The flu strain the Japanese government infected the dinosaurs with is genetically similar to the antdemic strain," Sims says. "It's entirely possible the antdemic is the result of our tampering with the natural order." Japanese officials refuted her claims with an official statement: "Dr. Sims's accusations are irresponsible and wholly without merit. The virus released in 2012 saved millions of lives." A World Health Organization investigation is pending.

wave hundreds of feet tall may be inviting, but it would be the last wave you'll ever ride," says Fin Shepard. "If the wave doesn't kill you, the dinosaurs will."

- **Grab ahold of something sturdy.** If you are caught in floodwaters, find something solid like a streetlight or a large tree to hold on to. Make sure what you're clutching isn't the neck of an apatosaurus.
- **Watch for multiple waves.** Each wave may bring new horrific dinosaurs, depending on its height and strength.
- **When a dinosaur attacks, fight back.** What else are you going to do? According to Hayato, small dinosaurs like velociraptors are vulnerable to gunshots and blunt-force trauma. An aluminum baseball bat works well and never runs out of ammo or gas.

NOTE: *In the rare situation a megatsunami washes a* T. rex *into your path, you won't be carrying a weapon large enough to hurt it. If it's intent on eating you, it will eat you. However, you will be killed by the coolest dinosaur ever. Most people go their whole lives without ever seeing a* T. rex *in person. Do you know how lucky you are?*

Carnivore or Herbivore?

One will eat your garden; one will eat your gardener. Identifying carnivorous dinosaurs could be the difference between life and death during a dinonami. Test your skills on these commonly cloned dinosaur species:

1. Tyrannosaurus
2. Triceratops
3. Apatosaurus
4. Velociraptor
5. Allosaurus
6. Iguanodon
7. Stegosaurus
8. Kosmoceratops
9. Spinosaurus
10. Brontosaurus

Answers: 1. Carnivore 2. Herbivore 3. Herbivore 4. Carnivore 5. Carnivore 6. Herbivore 7. Herbivore 8. Herbivore 9. Carnivore 10. Neither—the "brontosaurus" never existed, thus it can't be cloned

SHARKNADO

SHARKNADO

VITALS

ALSO KNOWN AS: Twister from Another Mister
FIRST OBSERVED: Los Angeles, California (2013) • **EST. MAX.
SPEED:** 70 mph (Swirling Wind up to 300 mph) • **HIGH-RISK
GROUPS:** Beach Bums, Bus Drivers, Best Friends • **LOOK OUT
FOR IT IN:** Open Saltwater, Coastal Regions • **THREAT TO
HUMANITY:** 💀💀💀 • **RISK OF ENCOUNTER:** 🦈🦈🦈 •
FIN'S WTF FACTOR: ⚠️⚠️⚠️⚠️

S YOU CAN GATHER FROM THE NAME, A SHARK-
nado is a tornado filled with sharks. These sharks
are extraordinarily aggressive, not because they're
hungry—they probably are—but because they're
angry and confused. You'd be in a bad mood too if
someone picked you up, spun you in circles at several hundred miles
an hour, and threw you through some stranger's living room window.

STUDY ■ ■ ■ IN 2013, HURRICANE David spawned three waterspouts off the California coast. The powerful aquatic tornados made a beeline for Los Angeles, sweeping up thousands of great whites, hammerheads, and tiger sharks in their path.

Scientists blame the irregular weather on climate change. Some fringe theorists, however, have posited that sharknados are government creations. "The government knows what we buy, what we eat, and where we go to the bathroom. They even know what kind of cheese I like ... pepper jack," says Beau Major, a part-time cashier at Burbank Liquor in Los Angeles. "They control it all, the weather too. I gotta hand it to them, though. Sharks—I never saw that coming."

Regardless of what caused them, the sharknados battered Los Angeles with their deadly cargo. Thousands of people died before Fin Shepard's son Matt and bartender Nova Clarke dropped bombs into the sharknados, dissipating two of the funnels. Unfortunately, Clarke fell out of a helicopter and into the waiting jaws of a massive great white.

Fin took care of the third and final sharknado. "I'm no hero," he says. "I'm just some guy who drove an SUV with a ticking bomb into a sharknado, chainsawed one of my employees [Clarke] out of a shark's belly, and saved a school bus full of children, one by one, from shark-infested floodwaters."

AVOID ■ ■ ■ THE KEY TO surviving a sharknado is being prepared for a sharknado.

- **Keep an eye out for inclement-weather alerts.**
  - **Sharknado watches** mean that conditions are favorable for a sharknado to occur (stormy conditions over a body of seawater coupled with abnormally large gatherings of sharks).
  - **Sharknado warnings** mean that an actual sharknado has been spotted. Sharks are flying through the freaking air.

How to Wield a Chainsaw Like a Boss

Chainsaws are great all-purpose tools for unnatural disasters. They're useful for cutting trees in the road, scaring your daughter's boyfriend, and—of course—killing sharks. When a great white is flying straight for you and you have one of these gasoline-powered bad boys in your hands, there's only one thing to do. Let 'er rip. User manual? More like "loser manual." Here's all you need to know.

1. If the chainsaw has a primer bulb, pump it three times.
2. If the chainsaw has a choke lever, place it into the "choke" position.
3. Activate the chain brake.
4. Switch it on.
5. With your left hand on the front handle and the back of the chainsaw between your legs or under your foot, pull the starter rope. If the engine doesn't start, try again.
6. Kneel on one knee and raise the chainsaw over your head. Use both hands. Point it toward the sky, angled back slightly. The shark's nose should hit it lengthwise—avoid using the tip of the chainsaw, as you may lose control.
7. If you are positioned properly, you will cut the shark in two right down the middle. The two halves should land on either side of you, leaving you bloody but unharmed.

- **Board up your windows.** If you survive a sharknado, the last thing you want is to come home to a tiger shark doing laps in your flooded family room. While you can't prevent water or wind damage, you can keep sharks at bay with some two-by-fours, a bag of nails, and a hammer. Board your windows as soon as a sharknado warning is issued.

SURVIVE ▪ ▪ ▪ DON'T JUST STAND around and wait for sharks to rain down on you. When a sharknado starts flinging sharks in your general direction, run.

DO: Watch out for other flying debris. Keep an eye out for trees, house siding, trash, and the occasional runaway Ferris wheel.

DON'T: Listen to the Red Cross. During tornados, the Red Cross recommends taking shelter in a basement, storm cellar, or interior room. Sharknados are a different beast. Because flash flooding occurs in conjunction with sharknados, your "safe place" in a basement or closet may be a) flooded and b) filled with hungry sharks.

DO: Drive fast and furious. Get as far away from the coast as you can. If a cop tries to pull you over, wave good-bye and press the nitrous button. One of you will be chum soon enough anyway. However, tornados have been clocked at over seventy miles per hour—easy enough to outrun on the open road, but impossible on the 405 during rush hour. Also, be advised that fins in the mirror are closer than they appear.

WHATEVER YOU DO, ABSOLUTELY DON'T: Hotwire a chopper and drop bombs into the sharknado. While enough heat will cause the funnel to dissipate, this is dangerous. Matt Shepard was lucky. Ninety-nine times out of a hundred, it's a suicide mission. If you disregard our advice, at least get your mother's permission first.

From the Kitchen of Nova Clarke
Grilled Shark Steak

Why I Love This Recipe: When I was seven, my grandpa took me
fishing on one of those day charter deals with his friends. The boat
went down. My grandfather put me inside this little life raft for
safety. Suddenly, all these sharks started swarming. By morning,
my grandfather . . . everyone . . . they were all gone. Six people
went into the water and one little girl came out. The sharks took the
rest. They took my grandfather. So I really hate sharks. Except on
my dinner plate . . . lightly seasoned.

Ingredients: 1 dead shark, 2 cups milk, 1 tbsp. lemon juice, salt and
black pepper to taste

1. Following the sharknado, the streets will be littered with sharks. FEMA will move in shortly to collect them, so don't waste time—find a nice-sized specimen and haul it home.* Also—and I can't stress this enough—make sure the shark is dead before trying to load it into the backseat of your Ford Focus. Nothing will spoil your appetite faster than a fatal shark bite.

2. Clean the fish and cut off a couple of one-inch-thick steaks. Don't forget to check the shark's belly for any survivors it may have swallowed whole!

3. Wash steaks thoroughly and place in a dish of milk. Let stand an hour or two.

4. Prepare your grill for medium-high heat. Pat steaks dry. Season with lemon juice, salt, and pepper.

5. Shark steaks should be grilled 10 minutes per inch of thickness (turning once to cook evenly), until the meat is opaque and flakes easily when tested with a fork. Who's the apex predator now? You are.

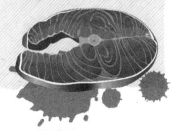

*Assuming your home wasn't destroyed.

WHALESTROM

WHALESTROM

HEN HUNDREDS OF WHALES CIRCLE A boat in the same direction, they cause a whalestrom—a massive whirlpool virtually impossible to escape. The whales (which can include prehistoric sperm whales, killer whales, and narwhals) circle because they think they've found something to eat, and they'll ram a boat to jolt prey loose, like when you shake a vending machine to knock a stuck Baby Ruth free. Fall overboard, and you're almost certainly dead.

STUDY ▪▪▪ WHALE WATCHING IS a lucrative business. It's also unpredictable. Dissatisfied customers are common. When too many negative reviews accumulate online, business goes down. That's the problem Regal Islands International executives faced in 2008 as their stock was tanking. If they could guarantee whale sightings on their cruises, they could turn business around.

Regal Islands scientists developed a solution. They created a beacon that broadcast a frequency mimicking an injured giant squid. On a live test run in Alaska's Glacier Bay, hundreds of killer whales answered the call. The school circled the cruise ship, delighting the passengers and, in turn, the executives. No one noticed the swirling water, however. No one except whale expert Nelson Reeves, who was fortuitously on his honeymoon aboard the cruise ship.

"The unprecedented number of orcas circling the boat created a whirlpool," he says. "Lurking amongst them was an enormous prehistoric sperm whale—a leviathan. It should have been extinct. Somehow, this beacon called it up from the depths."

The leviathan attacked the ship, knocking passengers overboard

CRAZY CONSPIRACY

Twenty million people cruise every year. If people know about whalestroms, why do they continue to put themselves in harm's way? Some critics say the industry isn't being forthright about the dangers associated with cruises. Survivor Wilma Summers shares the horrors she experienced on the boat—a "wretched death trap," in her words—in her *New York Times*-bestselling memoir *A Whale of a Bad Time: A Story of Survival* (an excerpt of which appears at the end of this guide). Industry spokesperson Rosalie Singleton refutes such claims. "Statistically speaking, cruise ships are the safest mode of transportation," she says. "You're more likely to be killed by a sasquatch while driving to the dock than you are by a whalestrom on your cruise."

into the waiting mouths of the hungry killer whales and damaging the ship's engine. Unable to escape the swirling waters, it began sinking into the whalestrom.

Reeves wrestled the beacon free from the executives and tossed it overboard into the leviathan's open mouth, causing the killer whales to descend on the prehistoric creature. "The beacon made the orcas think the leviathan was a wounded squid," Reeves says. "They tore him apart like kids opening presents on Christmas morning." As the whales stopped circling the boat, the whirlpool dissipated.

AVOID ▪▪▪ GOOD NEWS, LANDLUBBERS: Avoiding a whalestrom is as easy as never getting your feet wet. Whalestroms don't form on land. Even though whales can breathe air, you can't have a whirlpool without water.

SURVIVE ▪▪▪ YOU WENT OUT on a boat and got caught up in a whalestrom. Now what?

- **Attempt to navigate out of the whalestrom.** This sounds like common sense, but you'd be surprised how many people just freeze up. Unfortunately, in most cases it will be impossible to leave the whalestrom—especially if your boat is to blame.
- **Determine why you're the center of attention.** If the whales are circling your boat, find out why. If there's a beacon drawing them in, toss it overboard.
- **The whales may be hungry—so feed them.** Occasionally, whales will circle a boat because they're used to being fed by humans. If you're on a fishing boat, unload your catch. If you're on a cruise ship, throw that unfunny comedian overboard. He's had it coming for a long time.

When Earth Attacks

EXTREME-WEATHER VORTEX

EXTREME-WEATHER VORTEX

VITALS

ALSO KNOWN AS: Tornado Terror
FIRST OBSERVED: New York City, New York (2008) • **EST. MAX. SPEED:** 10 mph (Swirling Wind up to 100 mph) • **HIGH-RISK GROUPS:** Gawkers, Sightseers • **LOOK OUT FOR IT IN:** All Environments • **THREAT TO HUMANITY:** 💀💀💀 • **RISK OF ENCOUNTER:** 🌀🌀🌀🌀 • **FIN'S WTF FACTOR:** ⚠️⚠️

HILE VISUALLY SIMILAR IN SATELLITE photos to hurricanes, extreme-weather vortices are much more dangerous. Unlike hurricanes, these swirling storm systems are stationary. The chemical reactions inside these atmospheric mixing bowls cause unnatural phenomena like powerful upper-atmospheric lightning close to the ground and

ice twisters (see **ICE TWISTER**). These phenomena are fast-occurring, temporary or semipermanent, and impossible to predict. While vortices may be relatively new to our planet, they're common on other planets with disengaged high and low atmospheres. Jupiter's red spot vortex has been swirling over a fixed location for more than four hundred years.

STUDY ▪ ▪ ▪ ON THE MORNING of May 18, 2008, the air in the lower atmosphere above Manhattan began swirling. The brewing storm system went unnoticed by meteorologists, whose instruments track weather higher in the atmosphere.

The first sign of trouble happened in Central Park. Six-foot-tall whirlwinds filled with subzero air whipped through the park. Children chased these "mini tornados" around—until the tornados started chasing the kids back. The mini tornados soon merged into a full-scale ice twister, which threw one unlucky man sixty feet up into the air. A second ice twister formed near Liberty Island, killing dozens and ripping off the Statue of Liberty's raised arm.

"The devastation was just beginning. The ice twisters were the least of our worries," meteorologist Cassie Lawrence says. "At the site of one funnel touchdown in Midtown, I found evidence of lightning. It made perfect sense. Planets with high and low atmospheres are lightning machines. If the storm continued to build, I calculated the lightning would increase in frequency exponentially, building to a crescendo the likes of which we'd never seen on Earth before."

As Mother Nature put on a killer light show, Lawrence convinced city officials to load rockets with dry ice and shoot them into the extreme-weather vortex. The chemical reaction disrupted the storm system, putting an end to the ice twisters and lightning that had claimed thousands of lives.

New York State legislators proposed a law limiting the size of storm systems over the city. When critics argued that such an ordinance would be impossible to enforce, lawmakers dismissed their concerns. "With enough money, anything is possible," one prominent senator said. Weeks after the law passed, a New York state judge overturned it.

AVOID ▪▪▪ EXTREME-WEATHER VORTICES PRESENT multiple threats to your well-being. While ice twisters grab the headlines, the unnaturally powerful lightning is the real hazard. Lightning kills about seventy people a year in the United States—or it did until lightning from the New York City vortex killed many times that number in a single day. With that in mind, here's how to avoid becoming the next casualty.

- **Fortify your home against lightning.** Use surge protectors with all electronics. Install lightning rods on your home.
- **Fortify your body against lightning.** Remove all piercings (including that one your parents don't know about—you know which one we mean). Leave your watch on the nightstand. And it's time you retired that chain wallet, isn't it?

WEIRD SCIENCE

During the 2008 extreme-weather vortex above New York, many saw upper-atmospheric lightning for the first time. Upper-atmospheric lightning usually occurs above storm clouds and lasts only a few milliseconds, making it difficult to observe under normal conditions. In fact, the first visual evidence of upper-atmospheric lightning was recorded in 1989, when a space shuttle caught images of a ghostly "red sprite" over Australia. Other upper-atmospheric lightning that we'll start seeing thanks to vortices include strange phenomena like blue jets and ELVES (Emission of Light and Very low-frequency perturbations due to Electromagnetic pulse Sources—say that five times fast).

Extreme-Weather Vortices: Fact or Fiction?

Rubber-soled shoes will protect you from a lightning strike.
Fiction. While rubber is an insulator, it's not powerful enough to insulate you from lightning. Lightning bolts can burn through insulated power lines. Even if your shoes were ceramic, they would be of no help. Besides, ceramic shoes have terrible arch support.

If you're on a boat and have scuba gear, dive underwater for as long as possible.
Fact. You are safer underwater than being the tallest object on the open water. Since vortices tend to linger, however, this seems of limited use—you will run out of air at some point, long before the vortex runs out of lightning.

You are safer inside a car than outside one.
Fact. While a car's rubber tires do not provide protection against lightning strikes, cars can conduct lightning through their metal bodies. This disperses the electricity, possibly saving your life. No word on whether it's also a cheap way to charge an electric car.

SURVIVE ▪ ▪ ▪ TREAT THE EXTREME-WEATHER vortex as a threat until authorities have given you the "all clear." Over half of all lightning strikes occur after a storm has passed. Vortex-related phenomena are even more unpredictable.

If you're indoors:

- Get to the lowest floor of your building.
- Stay away from windows and doors.
- Do not use corded phones or cell phones—even for texting.

- Unplug anything connected to an electrical outlet, including appliances like air conditioners and computers.
- Keep your pets close by—outfit them in "thunder shirts" if possible to calm them.
- Avoid all plumbing—do not take a shower, wash your hands, or use the toilet. This could get messy.

If you're outdoors:

- Avoid anything tall that may attract lightning—trees, flagpoles, NBA players, etc.
- Avoid flimsy structures such as picnic shelters, baseball dugouts, and gazebos.
- Do not go swimming or boating.
- Avoid wide-open spaces like beaches—now is not the time for a romantic walk.

FIRENADO

FIRENADO

VITALS

ALSO KNOWN AS: Devil's Firestorm
FIRST OBSERVED: Tokyo, Japan (1923) • **EST. MAX. SPEED:**
20 mph (Wildfire), 60 mph (Storm Clouds), 160 mph (Swirling Wind)
• **HIGH-RISK GROUPS:** Hikers, Nature Lovers, Cowboys and
Cowgirls • **LOOK OUT FOR IT IN:** All Environments • **THREAT
TO HUMANITY:** 💀💀💀 • **RISK OF ENCOUNTER:** 🔥🔥🔥 •
FIN'S WTF FACTOR: ⚠️⚠️⚠️⚠️

FIRENADOS OCCUR WHEN TURBULENT AIR PASSES through wildfires, creating columns of fire. Funnels hundreds of feet wide and more than a thousand feet tall have been observed. The prolonged heat of wildfires occasionally generates storm clouds, resulting in rare top-down firenados. A single storm may spawn multiple long-lasting firenados, limited in destructive power only by the availability of material to burn.

STUDY ▪ ▪ ▪ WHILE FIRE IS a necessary part of the forest eco-system, wildfires aren't as welcome by people living near forests or grasslands. To prevent larger catastrophes, authorities sanction controlled burns.

Unfortunately, even the most carefully managed fires occasionally spread, threatening the same communities they're supposed to protect. Renewal is a great concept until it's your house that's "renewed." That's what happened in 2009 when the Colorado Forestry Service attempted to burn two hundred acres. Unexpectedly strong El Niño winds carried the fire past the prescribed boundaries. The heat created a storm system above the blaze, spawning firenados.

"Flames scorched half of Colorado Springs," says park ranger Miranda Conner. "My five-year-old suggested asking a superhero to freeze a lake with super breath and drop it onto the firenados. I told her this wasn't some comic book. People's lives were at stake. However, the more I thought about it, the more I realized it might actually work."

After Conner contacted a friend at the air force, a fleet of B-1 bombers airlifted glaciers from the Alaskan coast. The planes dropped their frozen cargo into the storm clouds, dousing the firenados. "Superheroes might not be real, but the US military is," Conner says.

AVOID ▪ ▪ ▪ STUDY THESE TIPS to be ready when the hellfire hits:

- **Plan multiple escape routes.** Find at least two different routes out of your neighborhood. Practice driving them every chance you get. This may confuse your neighbors. Wave to put them at ease.
- **Keep your yard tidy.** Fires need fuel to burn. Cut down on fuel sources in your yard. Water and mow your lawn. Rake up leaves. Pick up dead branches. You've been meaning to do this stuff for a while anyway, right?

Melting Points

The temperature inside a firenado funnel can exceed 2,000°F. That's hot enough to melt glass and many metals, including silver, bronze, and cast iron.

Metal	Fahrenheit
Washington Monument (Aluminum Cap)	1220°F
The *Rocky* Statue (Bronze)	1700°F
Brass Knuckles	1700 °F
Gold Wedding Band	1948°F
Statue of Liberty (Copper)	1984°F
St. Louis Gateway Arch (Stainless Steel)	2600°F

SURVIVE ▪ ▪ ▪ NOW THAT YOU'VE done all that yard work, we'll let you in on a secret: When a firenado occurs, you're safer outdoors.

- **First, get out of your home.** Then, stay as low to the ground as possible. If it's inevitable that the flames will catch up to you, find a ditch, drainage pipe, or other recessed area to lie down in. If your state is cash-strapped, you may even be able to find a pothole deep enough to hop into.
- **Stop, drop, and roll.** If your clothing catches fire, don't act like you're too cool to care. Stop whatever you're doing. Next, drop to the ground. Finally, roll around until the flames are extinguished.
- **Treat burns.** Wash the burn with water for three to five minutes. Do not break blisters. Cover the burn with a moist sterile bandage or cloth. Seek medical attention. Do not apply ice, ointments, or home remedies such as egg whites and butter. Who does that anyway? Egg whites? Everyone knows you're just supposed to use the yolk.

ICE TWISTER

ICE TWISTER

CE TWISTERS ARE FUNNELS FILLED WITH ICE CHUNKS AND subzero temperatures. If you're caught outside in their deadly path, you can be turned into a human Popsicle in under a minute. Even if you manage to avoid freezing to death, you still have to fend off flying ice and violent winds. Ice twisters can happen under any conditions, even on cloudless days.

STUDY ■■■ WHEN A RESEARCH team from the Federal Science Foundation (FSF) deployed thousands of experimental weather drones into the air over Oregon (a state that has long suffered from its lack of precipitation), they were attempting to make it rain—literally.

Operation R.A.I.N.D.A.N.C.E. was successful beyond their wildest dreams. New clouds formed, bringing rain to the Beaver State. However, their tampering also created deadly ice twisters that destroyed homes and froze victims solid. With the help of bestselling novelist Charlie Price (see the sidebar "An Interview with Charlie Price"), FSF researchers starved the storm system by heating the upper atmosphere. No more cold air, no more ice twisters.

FSF researcher Joanne Grant used federal whistleblower protections to testify before the House Committee on Unnatural Affairs. She accused FSF officials of ignoring internal warnings about possible unnatural phenomena caused by R.A.I.N.D.A.N.C.E. Her superiors allegedly knew about the threats and continued with the experiments anyway. They secretly hoped to use the technology to fight terrorism. "Ice twisters could be a pretty serious weapon if pointed in the right direction," she told the committee with a shiver. "Is it chilly in here, or is it just me?"

AVOID ▪ ▪ ▪ YOU NEVER KNOW when and where an ice twister will hit. Live your life in anticipation of the sudden onset of subzero temperatures.

- **Dress for cold weather like you mean it.** Wear layers of moisture-wicking clothing (wool, polypropylene, polyester thermal underwear). Clothing with a Gore-Tex shell will protect you from chilling winds. This could be a bit on the warm side, especially if you live in a moderate to tropical climate. Nevertheless, ask yourself: Would you rather be sweating balls, or frozen stiff like a caveman in a glacier? Unlike Encino Man, you can't be warmed back to life.

How to Pass Time During a Storm

You could be stuck indoors for several hours. If the ice twisters are part of an extreme-weather vortex, you're looking at several days. So what do you and your family do in the meantime? If your electricity is out, your options are severely limited—no cable TV or Netflix. Here's what we suggest:

- Play cards—poker, Uno, or Cards Against Humanity.
- Read a book—the one you're reading now works quite nicely, unless you've bought the electronic or audio edition.
- Exercise—push-ups, pull-ups, that sort of thing.
- Sing songs.
- Play board games— Parcheesi, Risk, Monopoly.
- Put together an elaborate puzzle (1,000 pieces or more).
- Eat everything in your freezer or refrigerator—without electricity, it's going to spoil anyway.
- Two words: MAKEOUT TIME!

- **Always protect your head.** Wearing a helmet is a no-brainer. Your skull is strong, but a chunk of ice traveling at 200 mph is stronger. When a freak ice twister hits some Saturday afternoon, you'll be glad you wore that bicycle helmet to the mall.

- **Drive a heavy-duty pickup.** If you're not willing to dress for an ice twister at all times (and let's face it, we don't blame you), then at least have a vehicle capable of withstanding one. You'll want a large pickup, the kind you see advertised during NFL games. Get the optional LINE-X weather coating, which is the same element-resistive coating used on US Navy ships, SWAT vehicles, and Guy Fieri's hair.

SURVIVE ▪▪▪ GRAB SOME BLANKETS and winter clothing, and then follow the usual tornado safety precautions.

DO: Get inside to the basement or lowest floor. Find an interior room away from windows. If you're in an office building, gather with your coworkers in a restroom. That's always a good time. Totally not awkward for anybody.

DON'T: Huddle down in a corner. They're among the least safe places to wait out tornados. Likewise, avoid hunkering down in the basement directly below a large object on the first floor. Being crushed by a piano is funny on *Looney Tunes*. In real life, it's hilarious.

DO: Stay in your car if you can't get safely to a building. If you have an open road, gun it—you may be able to outrun the ice twister. If the road isn't clear, pull over. Place your head between your legs and cover the back of your neck with your hands. Don't forget to buckle your seatbelt just in case you go airborne.

DON'T: Park underneath an overpass. Many people assume an overpass provides protection during tornados. They assume wrong. Overpasses attract more debris and stronger winds than open areas. See what can happen when you make assumptions?

WEIRD SCIENCE

Scientists have been trying to make it rain by seeding clouds with chemicals for over a century. Sometimes it works; sometimes it doesn't. The FSF researchers went a step further. Instead of seeding clouds, they created them. Using experimental drones outfitted with revolutionary moisture evaporators, researchers condensed liquid nitrogen out of the upper atmosphere and pushed it downward, resulting in moisture-rich clouds. That should guarantee them a blue ribbon at their next science fair.

An Interview with Charlie Price, the *New York Times*–bestselling Author of *Ionos-fear*

To the FSF researchers' dismay, the ice twisters were headed straight for Portland, the home of hipsters, Powell's Books, and the world's first and only vegan strip club. Out of ideas, FSF's Joanne Grant enlisted the aid of an old colleague, bestselling novelist Charlie Price. Using a solution straight out of one of Price's books, they stopped the storm before it could turn Portland into Iceland.

You used to be a scientist. Why did you trade science fact for science fiction?

I got tired of sitting around waiting on funding. I got sick of kowtowing to the whims of politicians more worried about reelection campaigns than the environment.

Did you ever think the solutions offered by the characters in your books would really work?

No. I never even expected the ice twisters in *Ionos-fear* would become a reality—at least not within my lifetime. Who knew the solution I created in my book would actually work in real life? Heating the upper atmosphere with low-orbit satellites is just nuts. [laughs] I'm no scientist. I'm just a writer blessed with the luxury of dreaming up disasters.

Some reviewers have criticized your books as apocalyptic.

Everyone's worried about sharknados right now, after what happened in Los Angeles. I take real-life threats like that and try to imagine scenarios even more grim. What if you're an astronaut, and get caught outside the shuttle during a meteor shower? What if you're not alone? What if there are sharks? That's where *Space Sharknado* came from. Apocalyptic? Maybe. But that's what sells these days.

See **APPENDIX: SPACE SHARK-NADO** *for an excerpt from Price's forthcoming novel,* Space Sharknado.

METEOR STORM

METEOR STORM

VITALS

ALSO KNOWN AS: Space Rocks
FIRST OBSERVED: San Francisco, California (2010) •
EST. MAX. SPEED: 160,000 mph • **HIGH-RISK GROUPS:**
Hippies, Techies, Trekkies • **LOOK OUT FOR IT IN:** All Environments
• **THREAT TO HUMANITY:** 💀💀💀 • **RISK OF ENCOUNTER:** 🔥🔥
• **FIN'S WTF FACTOR:** ⚠️⚠️

HILE THE METEOROIDS ENTERING EARTH'S atmosphere during a meteor shower leave behind brilliant streaks of light, most are no bigger than a grain of sand. Meteor storms, on the other hand, feature hefty rocks made of robust elements capable of passing through the atmosphere without burning up. Aided by gravity and a depleted ozone layer, these meteorites can strike the Earth's surface at speeds of more than 100,000 mph. At that speed, even a marble-sized rock is capable of drilling a hole through your roof—to say nothing of your cranium.

STUDY ▪ ▪ ▪ WHAT WAS SUPPOSED to be an intense but beautiful display in 2010 turned deadly as thousands of unbinilium meteorites from the comet Leder-Bay rained down on San Francisco. KGSF-13 news anchor Kyle Kemper described the scene following Meteor Storm Geordi as a war zone.

Over the next eight hours, three additional meteor storms hit San Francisco. "Because of our planet's rotation and orbit, the additional storms should have been spread out across the globe," astronomer Dr. Michelle Young says. "Unfortunately, unbinilium deposits in San Francisco Bay acted as an air traffic controller, guiding the meteorites toward the city. Unbinilium builds up electrostatic attraction and eventually discharges it. It's not magnetism, but that's the closest analogue. It's more like my relationship with my ex-husband."

Once the fourth storm (Meteor Storm Jean-Luc) ended, Dr. Young realized Earth wasn't free and clear just yet. An asteroid, cloaked by the unbinilium meteoroids, was on a collision course with Earth.

Dr. Young and government officials devised a last-minute plan incorporating cutting-edge and untested technology. They detonated 1.2-megaton B-83 nuclear warheads near the rogue asteroid, diverting its path. "We got extremely lucky," Dr. Young says. "And I'm not just talking about the Giants winning the World Series that year."

AVOID ▪ ▪ ▪ IF YOU EVER find yourself under siege by a meteor storm, ducking under your kitchen table won't cut it. You need a fallout shelter that meets the following specifications:

- 20 feet underground
- Concrete walls and ceiling (2 feet thick)
- 10 x 10 feet for up to six occupants (add 2.5 feet in length for each additional person)

WEIRD SCIENCE

Meteoroids are rocks traveling through space. **Meteors** are the flashes of light as the meteoroids hit the Earth's atmosphere (also known as shooting stars). **Meteorites** are meteoroids that make it through the atmosphere. Got that? There will be a quiz later.

- Ventilation with filters to collect debris and dust
- Electrical, Internet, and cable hookups

Grab a case of beer and a few shovels, invite some friends over, and start digging.

SURVIVE ■ ■ ■ TAKE REFUGE IN your fallout shelter. You built one like we suggested, right? No? Don't despair. There's still hope.

- **Set down the rocket launcher.** Don't attempt to shoot meteorites out of the air. Such an attempt would be beyond foolish. Even if you somehow locked your missile on a single meteorite and scored a direct hit, the most it would do is shatter it, scattering debris over a much larger area—and increasing the likelihood a fragment will strike you.
- **You're no safer indoors.** As the heavens rain down around you, having a roof over your head is reassuring. However, it's an illusion of comfort—nothing more. Support beams and foundations can be weakened by meteorite strikes, causing buildings to collapse without warning.
- **Stay still for just one ever-loving moment.** Every time there's a meteor storm, people begin running around in zigzag patterns. Sit down. You cannot outrun meteorites. You're better off conserving your energy, in case you need to save your daughter's boyfriend from a pile of rubble. Then again, maybe not. Depends what you think of the boy.

POLAR STORM

POLAR STORM

VITALS

ALSO KNOWN AS: Magnetic Mayhem
FIRST OBSERVED: Fairbanks, Alaska (2009) • **EST. MAX. SPEED**: N/A • **HIGH-RISK GROUPS**: Human Beings Who Live on Earth • **LOOK OUT FOR IT IN**: All Environments • **THREAT TO HUMANITY**: 💀💀💀💀💀 • **RISK OF ENCOUNTER**: ⚡⚡ • **FIN'S WTF FACTOR**: ⚠️⚠️⚠️⚠️⚠️

CCASIONALLY, A METEORITE SO LARGE MAKES IT through Earth's atmosphere that the impact tilts the planet's axis. This causes the magnetic poles to begin the slow but painful process of switching places—a "polar storm." North becomes south, and vice versa. "That doesn't sound so bad," you say. "I can't remember the last time I used a compass." And it might not be so bad . . . if that was all that happened. Within days of the planet being knocked out of alignment, earthquakes begin happening worldwide. New magnetic fields ("mini poles") spontaneously form and spread around

the globe. These mini poles discharge electromagnetic shockwaves, which fry electronics—and anyone using them—for hundreds of miles in all directions. Lastly, the Earth's magnetic shield—the one that protects us from solar radiation—becomes weaker the further the polar storm progresses. Without it, humanity is doomed.

STUDY ▪ ▪ ▪ IN 2009, A small fragment broke away from the comet Copernicus and hurtled toward Earth. While much of it burned up in the atmosphere, a chunk measuring three hundred meters wide made landfall near Alaska. A quarter of a million people expired in the fallout.

"My science advisors have reported that the immediate crisis is over. The American people are safe and can go on with their lives," President Obama said in a televised press conference forty-eight hours after the incident.

However, the Storm Hazard Research Center's James Mayfield believed the threat wasn't over. He pointed to an apparent shift in the Earth's axis as the beginning of the end for life on Earth. White House advisors initially dismissed Mayfield's prediction of a complete pole reversal as an attempt to incite mass hysteria. They labeled him a national security threat. "That hurt, but I've been called worse," Mayfield says.

WEIRD SCIENCE

The Earth's magnetic field has reversed thousands of times throughout history because of changes in the Earth's iron-laden molten core. The poles switch places about once every 400,000 years, according to Mayfield. The most recent reversal was 780,000 years ago. In the past ten years, the North Pole has been observed moving from Canada toward Russia at a rate of forty miles per year. Either it's defecting from NATO, or we're looking at the early stages of a pole reversal.

When images of destruction caused by the mini poles and earthquakes began appearing, the White House changed course. Under Mayfield's direction, a submarine dropped two fifty-megaton bombs into the Southern Hemisphere's Mariana Trench. The implausible gambit worked, shocking the planet back into alignment. But you already guessed that. If the plan hadn't succeeded, you wouldn't be around to read about it.

AVOID ▪ ▪ ▪ ASTRONOMERS HAVE ASSURED the public that we're in the clear as far as near-Earth objects go for the immediate future. Of course, that was also what they said before the Copernicus fragment hit us. Prepare for earthquakes and mini poles now.

How to Orient Yourself Without a Compass

During a polar storm, your compass is about as worthless as a TV without a remote. Your only hope is to navigate using the sun, moon, and stars.

1. Find a straight, thin stick and flat ground.
2. Jam the stick into the ground at 9 a.m. Mark where the tip of the shadow falls.
3. Wait until 3 p.m. Mark where the tip of the shadow falls.
4. Draw a line between the two points. This is the west/east line.
5. The north/south line can be found by making a right angle on the west/east line.
6. Realize that your homemade compass is just giving you the same janky readings your magnetic compass gave you. The position of the sun, moon, and stars is meaningless after the axial shift. We're idiots and didn't think this through all the way. Sorry about that.

- **Ensure your home is built to seismic codes.** If you rent, check with your landlord. They'll probably blow you off. How long's it been since you notified them of that leak in your bathroom ceiling? That still isn't fixed? Oh dear.

- **What's on the walls is as potentially dangerous as the walls themselves.** Move bookshelves away from couches and chairs. Don't hang anything above your headboard, unless you want to be killed during the night by that framed Benedict Cumberbatch poster. Not a bad way to go, honestly.

- **Drop off the grid.** To be safe from the next mini-pole electrical storm, ditch your cell phone. Unplug from the Internet. Live a quiet, peaceful life like one of those sensitive literary writer types. You can still have fun without electricity—pick up a pair of binoculars and go bird-watching.

Electronics to Avoid During Polar Storms

- Planes, trains, and automobiles
- Cell phones and MP3 players
- Google Glasses
- Segways
- Laptops, computers, and tablets
- Blenders and juicers
- Hair dryers, curling irons, and hair straighteners
- Roombas
- Treadmills and exercise bikes
- High-fidelity stereo equipment
- Drones
- Heated Aqua-Jet Foot Spas
- Electric toothbrushes and razors
- Furbies and other battery-powered children's toys
- Cordless weed whackers and other garden tools*

*In fact, you should probably avoid doing yard work during a polar storm. Not only is it dangerous, but there's a good chance you'll be dead within the week anyway. Contemplating your own mortality while mowing the lawn is less fun than it sounds.

SURVIVE ▪ ▪ ▪ DURING A POLAR storm, multiple unnatural disasters may happen simultaneously.

- **In the event of a polar storm–related earthquake, drop to the ground until the initial tremors pass.** Not even a world-champion surfer like Fin Shepard can stay upright and balanced during a major earthquake.
- **As soon as the ground stops shaking, get indoors.** Avoid huddling in doorways. You should be safe from aftershocks under a sturdy table. Yet another reason to get a real dining room table in place of the card table you've been using since college.
- **Don't smoke.** Busted gas lines are common during earthquakes. Unless you want to blow up, put down the cigarette. You've been meaning to quit for a while anyway, right?
- **If you can't get out of Dodge, get out of your Dodge.** Cars are particularly unsafe during polar storms. Your car probably won't turn on—and if it does, you run the risk of electrocution.
- **If you have a solution, speak up.** Unless the polar storm is stopped, we will eventually be left defenseless against cosmic radiation. There's no way to survive if things progress that far. If you have any ideas about how to fix the planet's alignment, don't hesitate to call or tweet your congressperson. No idea is too wild. In 2009, we dropped nuclear bombs into the ocean. Seriously.

STONADO

STONADO

TONADO FUNNELS ARE POWERFUL ENOUGH TO lift a four-ton rock into the air. The more dangerous threat, however, are the softball-sized "rocks" the storm system creates in the upper atmosphere. These rocks are actually ozone droplets frozen in carbon dioxide. After forming, the ozone rocks descend into the funnels that hurl them in all directions at mind-boggling speeds. As soon as they hit the ground, atmospheric pressure causes them to explode.

STUDY ■ ■ ■ IN 2013, AN extreme-weather vortex (see **EXTREME-WEATHER VORTEX**) descended upon Massachusetts. One funnel associated with the storm picked up the historic 8,000-pound Plymouth Rock and deposited it nearly forty miles away onto a Boston basketball court. Soon, rocks were flying all around Beantown.

"At first, we thought the funnels were just picking rocks up off the ground. Tornados pick up things all the time—look at the sharknados," Boston weatherman Lee Carlton says. "Unfortunately, we quickly learned the storm system was also creating rocks. The vortex kicked ozone into the upper atmosphere, where it froze and descended back to Earth as frozen rocks."

With the city under siege, Carlton and his storm-chasing brother devised a plan to stop the stonados that included loading an experimental five-ton warhead into their SUV and driving it into one of the stonado funnels (leaping out at the last second, of course). When the stonado swept the SUV into the air, the bomb exploded—igniting the hydrogen in the lower atmosphere, which temporarily raised the local temperature and choked the stonados out.

HIDDEN HISTORY

Although a stonado destroyed Plymouth Rock, it wasn't as big a loss for American history as you might think. Contrary to popular belief, the *Mayflower* never landed at the rock displayed as "Plymouth Rock." In fact, Pilgrim William Bradford never mentioned landing at *any* rock in his journal. A town elder "identified" Plymouth Rock in 1741—more than 120 years after the Pilgrims landed. "We have a team piecing it back together," museum curator Mead White says. "It's like a four-ton Rubik's Cube." He expects to complete the restoration sometime within the next ten to fifteen years. A lot of work for a fake piece of history, if you ask us.

AVOID ▪ ▪ ▪ STONADOS CAN HAPPEN without warning. One minute it could be raining; the next the sun is shining. It's almost like living in Colorado.

• **Always carry a barometer.** The barometric pressure changes rapidly just before a stonado forms. With a barometer, you can at least have a heads-up. While a high-end model like the Digiquartz Portable Model 765 barometric-pressure sensor might be out of your price range, more basic models are available on the cheap.

• **Buy full-coverage auto insurance.** If your car is parked outside during a stonado, it's going to get a few dings in the roof. In fact, you'd be lucky to still have a roof. Full-coverage insurance will protect your ride from stonados and other unnatural disasters.

SURVIVE ▪ ▪ ▪ IS A FUNNEL beginning to form overhead? Your survival depends upon how fast you can move. Even if you've got seats on the Green Monster for game seven of the American League playoffs against the Yankees, get to safety. Don't wait around to see if the game will be called.

• **Stay away from the unstable frozen rocks.** If one lands near you, hustle in the other direction. It's a ticking time bomb. It may be seconds or hours before it goes off—but when it does, you'll want to be at least twenty yards away. If it explodes behind you, leap in the air and make a dramatic movie-star landing.

• **Do we even have to say it? Get inside!** While stonado rocks aren't traveling as fast as meteorites, they're still going to smash through your North Face jacket. Get to the lowest floor of your building or the nearest stonado shelter.

STONEHENGE APOCALYPSE

STONEHENGE APOCALYPSE

VITALS

ALSO KNOWN AS: The New Dawn

FIRST OBSERVED: Wiltshire, England (2010) • **EST. MAX. SPEED:** N/A • **HIGH-RISK GROUPS:** Anyone Who Doesn't Join the New Dawn Doomsday Cult • **LOOK OUT FOR IT IN:** All Environments • **THREAT TO HUMANITY:** 💀💀💀💀💀 • **RISK OF ENCOUNTER:** ⚡⚡ • **FIN'S WTF FACTOR:** ⚠️⚠️⚠️⚠️⚠️

F YOU THINK STONEHENGE IS JUST A QUIRKY COLLECTION of upright rocks, think again. Some scientists believe that the iconic obelisks are part of an ancient terraforming ("Earth-shaping") device that made the planet habitable for the first single-celled organisms. If activated today, however, Stonehenge would revert the Earth back to its earliest state through a series of supervolcanoes, earthquakes, and colossal floods.

STUDY ■ ■ ■ IN 2010, MEMBERS of the New Dawn doomsday cult foolishly turned Stonehenge on, beginning the terraforming process. "Civilization is a failed experiment," says one cult member, who asked his name be withheld. "If Stonehenge had been allowed to continue its mission, the air would be clean. The water would be fresh. It would have been a New Dawn."

Simultaneous volcanic eruptions and flooding in Mexico, Egypt, and Indonesia killed millions. With the clock ticking, *The Real Story* talk radio host Jacob Glaser managed to best the doomsday cult and shut Stonehenge down using the Antikythera mechanism. "It's the key that can turn Stonehenge on and off," explains the cult member. "I wish we had made a copy."

While we know the purpose of the megaliths, who built them is still a mystery. Noted astrobiologist Nigel St. Hubbins believes he knows the answer. "A strange alien race known as druids created Stonehenge," he says. "They're long gone, but their legacy remains—at least at renaissance fairs."

AVOID ■ ■ ■ UNLESS YOU'RE WILLING to invest billions of dollars in an infrastructure that generates breathable air, only one place can withstand the Stonehenge Apocalypse: the New Dawn's hidden pyramid shelter in Maine known as the Primordial Hill. While we're not saying you should join their cult, at least check out the pyramid's amenities:

- Wireless High-speed Internet Access
- Hair Dryers
- Cable TV, including HBO and Showtime
- Room Safes
- 24-hour Fitness Center

- Laundry
- Valet Parking
- Business Center
- In-room Dining
- Concierge Service
- Complimentary Bottled Water and *USA Today*

SURVIVE ■■■ ONCE THE TERRAFORMING process begins, you have two options.

1. **Seek shelter at the Primordial Hill.** You *did* join the New Dawn, right? Good. Then kick back and prepare for the end of the world. If you didn't join the cult, skip to step two.

2. **Use the Antikythera mechanism to shut Stonehenge down.** We're not sure it works (or even what it looks like), but you can probably find the instructions online.

Apocalyptic Drinks

While you're chilling in the pyramid shelter, you might want to pour out a drink in honor of all your friends and family who didn't heed your warning about the impending doom. Here are a few apocalyptic shots to drink in their honor.*

- **Four Horsemen.** 1 part Jim Beam bourbon whiskey, 1 part Jack Daniel's Tennessee whiskey, 1 part Johnnie Walker Black Scotch whiskey, and 1 part Jameson Irish whiskey. Mix all four together in a shot glass.
- **Nuclear Rainbow.** ½ oz. grenadine syrup, ½ oz. peppermint liqueur, ½ oz. Jägermeister, ½ oz. melon liqueur, ½ oz. Canadian whiskey, ½ oz. 151 rum, ½ oz. almond liqueur. Pour each over a spoon into a shot glass carefully, which will provide the layered "rainbow" effect.
- **Apocalypse Now.** ⅓ oz. dry vermouth, ⅓ oz. Irish cream liqueur, ⅓ oz. tequila. Pour vermouth and tequila into a cocktail shaker filled with ice. Shake well. Strain into shot glass. Top with Irish cream.

*Even during the end of the world, you must be twenty-one and older to drink in the United States. Drinking ages vary elsewhere. Always designate a driver and drink responsibly.

SWAMP VOLCANO

SWAMP VOLCANO

VITALS

ALSO KNOWN AS: Submarine Supervolcano
FIRST OBSERVED: Gulf of Mexico (2011) • **EST. MAX. SPEED:**
500 mph • **HIGH-RISK GROUPS:** DJs, Former Supermodels •
LOOK OUT FOR IT IN: Open Saltwater, Coastal Regions •
THREAT TO HUMANITY: 💀💀💀 • **RISK OF ENCOUNTER:**
⚡⚡⚡⚡ • **FIN'S WTF FACTOR:** ⚠️⚠️⚠️

THE FIRST SIGN OF AN ACTIVE SWAMP VOLCANO IS usually an earthquake, indicating an underwater volcanic eruption. The quake is followed closely by a wave of super-heated, skin-melting gas—a "steam tsunami." The destruction doesn't stop there. Lava flows swiftly through underground tunnels, making landfall in swampland hundreds of miles from the eruption. Glowing orange lava can reach temperatures of 1,600°F or higher. Even a brief touch is enough to leave a nasty burn. Fall in, and you'll go up in smoke in seconds.

STUDY ▪ ▪ ▪ ON MAY 23, 2011, an American oil company drilling deep in the Gulf of Mexico inadvertently triggered Swamp Volcano Levin, the first swamp volcano to erupt on American soil.

"Holter Energy was pumping millions of gallons of heated water deep into the ocean floor—a drilling process known as 'fracking'," University of Miami volcanologist Antoinette Vitrini explained to Congress in the subsequent hearings. "This heated the magma in the submarine supervolcano, triggering the eruption. While it may have eventually happened without human interference, Holter undoubtedly added fuel to the fire. No pun intended."

The steam tsunami slammed into the coast of southern Florida, killing hundreds. The worst was yet to come. The volcano was connected via prehistoric conduits to Miami—on the opposite side of the state. Mayhem ensued. The Everglades boiled, and lava flooded the streets of Miami. At Vitrini's suggestion, the military used liquid nitrogen to form a "cold cap" underground. This diverted the lava into Biscayne Bay, effectively ending the threat.

AVOID ▪ ▪ ▪ THE FARTHER INLAND you live, the greater your probability of survival. But if you go too far inland—to, say, Wyoming—all you've done is moved from one supervolcanic threat to another (see the sidebar "Volcanoes vs. Supervolcanoes"). Our advice? Stay put. Learn the signs of an eruption, so you can act when the time comes.

- **Is it snowing ash?** That's not a good sign. While it might not be a swamp volcano, *something* has erupted.
- **Did a steam tsunami melt your face off?** Probably a swamp volcano.
- **Is lava flooding out of storm drains?** Yep. Swamp volcano.

Volcanoes vs. Supervolcanoes

What's the difference between a volcano and a "supervolcano"? If you said one was from Krypton, you're wrong. Without getting overly technical, supervolcanoes are just big-ass volcanoes. Lake Toba, the last supervolcano to occur aboveground, erupted about 74,000 years ago in Indonesia, ushering in a 1,000-year-long period of cooled temperature. Here are five others to watch for.

- **Aira Caldera**—Kyūshū, Japan
- **Long Valley Caldera**—Mono County, California, USA
- **Taupo Caldera**—Lake Taupo, North Island, New Zealand
- **Valles Caldera**—Sandoval County, New Mexico, USA
- **Yellowstone Caldera**—Yellowstone National Park, Wyoming, USA

SURVIVE ■ ■ ■ BECAUSE SWAMP VOLCANOES occur with little warning, they are one of Mother Nature's most insidious unnatural disasters.

- **If a wall of super-heated gas is shooting toward you, duck underwater until it passes.** The steam travels over the surface of the water, not under it. Depending on how long you can hold your breath, you might be able to survive. You might also drown—six of one, half a dozen of the other.

- **Don't drive through lava.** Even if it appears shallow, no amount of lava is safe to drive through. If you're trapped in a vehicle surrounded by lava, crawl out the windows and onto the roof. Phone emergency services. There's a (slim) chance the lava could ignite your gas tank while you're hanging out on the roof. Talk about going out with a bang.

PART TWO
MONSTERS

Death If by
Land

BASILISK

BASILISK

VITALS

ALSO KNOWN AS: Serpent King
FIRST OBSERVED: Buffalo Springs, Colorado (2006) • **EST. MAX. SPEED:** 30 mph • **HIGH-RISK GROUPS:** Archaeologists, Enemies of the Order of the Sun • **LOOK OUT FOR IT IN:** Libya • **THREAT TO HUMANITY:** 💀💀 • **RISK OF ENCOUNTER:** 🦠🦠 • **FIN'S WTF FACTOR:** ⚠️⚠️⚠️⚠️

CCORDING TO LEGEND, THE FIRST BASILISK WAS hatched from a serpent egg by a male chicken. While the story is likely apocryphal, the monster itself is quite real. Its serpentine body is approximately fifteen feet long, with four unusable twig-like arms. Despite being called the "serpent king," the basilisk's head more closely resembles that of the long-extinct dragon. If it attacks you, it will first spit paralyzing venom on you. Once you're incapacitated, it locks eyes with you. It's not falling in love—it's turning you to stone. If the basilisk is in a hurry, it's liable to just snap your head off your body with its enormous jaws.

STUDY ■ ■ ■ "PEOPLE ASSUME BEING an archaeologist is like *Indiana Jones,*" University of Colorado professor Harry McColl says. "I used to say it's more rocks, less whips. Until I unearthed the basilisk in Libya, of course."

McColl was on a sponsored dig in 2006 when tribal leaders warned them to leave. "Much blood has been spilled here. Yours will be too if you do not leave this place and all you find behind. No man lives here. Only a great evil," McColl quotes the local emissary as saying. "We thought they were jealous. We'd just uncovered the statue of the basilisk and a five-foot gold-plated scepter topped with the head of a snake and a priceless jewel—the fabled 'Eye of Medusa.' An ancient cult—the Order of the Sun—used the scepter to control the basilisk." McColl ignored the warnings.

While the find was on display at the Buffalo Springs Museum of Natural History in Colorado, the jewel-encrusted scepter refracted light from a solar eclipse onto the basilisk statue—waking the monster within. The "statue" was a tomb meant to keep the dangerous animal locked up. The basilisk roared to life. Dozens were killed.

The basilisk escaped into the sewers, but not for long. The stage was set for McColl to step into Harrison Ford's fedora and save the day. He used the scepter to lure the basilisk inside a nuclear power plant. McColl believed the blue glow seen inside nuclear reactors (Cherenkov radiation, a byproduct of nuclear fission) would be enough to simulate another solar eclipse. Sure enough, the Eye of Medusa refracted light from the cooling tanks onto the basilisk, turning the creature back to stone. It's enough to make you wonder how many other statues are stone crypts housing living creatures. *Et tu,* President Lincoln?

AVOID ■ ■ ■ SCANS OF THE creature's body revealed it was pregnant, indicating that another basilisk must have existed at the time of its entombment. McColl and his team of historians are combing through myths, legends, and historical literature for clues to the whereabouts of more basilisks. Since the creature appears in literature throughout Asia and Europe right up until the Middle Ages, they aren't limiting their search to Libya. In the meantime, do what you can to avoid basilisks by using common sense.

- **Cancel any scheduled archaeological digs in Libya.** Just to be on the safe side.
- **Exercise caution around basilisk statues.** While we're sure it's a lovely city, avoid Basel, Switzerland, at all costs. The basilisk is the town's heraldic animal. Thirty-odd statues appear around town—possibly ready to come to life at any moment, given the right astronomical conditions.

SURVIVE ■ ■ ■ THINK YOU'RE POWERLESS against a creature as fearsome and indestructible as a basilisk? For the most part, that's true. Still, knowledge is power. Here's what works, and what doesn't. **DO: Avert your eyes.** If it doesn't lock eyes with you, it can't turn you to stone. Unfortunately, it can still rip you apart between its jaws.

WEIRD SCIENCE

Being turned to stone by a basilisk is nothing like being frozen in carbonite. When a basilisk stares into your eyes, your skin and organs transform into a mixture of limonite and silicate. If someone attempted "chipping you out" of the stone, they would eventually reach bone. Depending upon what you're wearing and what position you're in when turned to stone, you might at least make a fetching lawn ornament.

DON'T: Honk your horn or hold up a mirror. Some myths say that the basilisk can be driven away by loud noises. Others say that if the basilisk sees its own reflection, it will turn to stone like a manticore (see **MANTICORE**). The Colorado National Guard learned the hard way that neither of these stories holds any truth.

DO: Try to subdue it with the Eye of Medusa. Not only can the jewel wake the basilisk during an eclipse, it can also return it to its stone slumber under the same conditions. For unknown reasons, the basilisk is drawn to it. "Sometimes, we're drawn to what causes us pain. We don't always make rational decisions," McColl muses. The scepter is currently on display at the Museum of Libya in Tripoli.

DON'T: Shoot it or try to blow it up. Conventional weapons can't penetrate the beast's thick body armor. It survived a fiery inferno inside an exploding building, indicating it is also impervious to high temperatures. It's either the Eye of Medusa or nothing if you want to stop a basilisk.

Mythological Monsters

"History and myth go hand in hand. Witches, ghosts, and legendary creatures are often symbolic representations of mankind's ongoing quest to offset the ordinary of this world by seeking the extraordinary in another," McColl says. "I never considered the basilisk was real until the moment it came to life. Now I can't stop worrying about what mythological creature we'll see next." Here are a few that keep him up at night.

- **Chupacabra**—These legendary cryptids are allegedly native to the Americas. They feed on livestock by draining their victim's blood. While most skeptics believe chupacabras are coyotes and other dogs infected with mange, McColl isn't so sure. "The chupacabra is described as three or four feet tall, with red eyes and a forked tongue," he says. "That doesn't sound like any dogs that I know. Maybe a mutant vampire bat. Maybe."
- **Thunderbird**—Reports of large winged reptiles date back hundreds of years in North America. "It's easy to dismiss these accounts as cases of mistaken identity. But the fact of the matter is, pterosaurs like the pterodactyl are no myth," McColl says. "They flew through the skies once upon a time. Who's to say they still don't?"
- **Unicorn**—While generally presented as benign creatures in children's stories, McColl worries that a real-life encounter with a wild unicorn would be anything but magical. "Horses can be extremely aggressive creatures. There's no reason to believe unicorns would be any different. In 2010, for instance, two stampeding horses killed one person and hurt twenty-three others at an Iowa parade," he says. "Imagine the damage they could have done if they had foot-long horns jutting out of their foreheads."

BIGFOOT

BIGFOOT

VITALS

ALSO KNOWN AS: Sasquatch
FIRST OBSERVED: Deadwood, South Dakota (2012) • **EST. MAX. SPEED:** 25 mph • **HIGH-RISK GROUPS:** Shock Rockers, Partridges, Bradys • **LOOK OUT FOR IT IN:** US (Black Hills to the Pacific Northwest), Canada • **THREAT TO HUMANITY:** 💀 • **RISK OF ENCOUNTER:** 💥💥 • **FIN'S WTF FACTOR:** ⚠️⚠️⚠️

FORGET THE BIGFOOT OF LEGEND. REAL SASQUATCHES are much bigger—over two stories tall, making them the largest of the great apes. They live in mountainous regions of North America, where they subsist on a varied diet of root vegetables and small game. While they are generally docile, zoologists believe that humanity may have finally encroached too far upon their territory. When they attack people, they don't play around. They'll either snap your neck or bite your head off.

STUDY ■ ■ ■ INCONTROVERTIBLE PROOF OF the creature's existence comes to us from a 2012 rock concert in South Dakota, where a sasquatch was caught on film by dozens of attendees. Video from the event makes the classic Patterson film—the shaggy, man-sized beast swinging its arms in the woods—seem downright quaint. One shocking video from Deadwood shows the two-story sasquatch punting rocker Alice Cooper a hundred yards over the heads of fleeing concertgoers. The video has over 100 million views on YouTube.

"Mother Nature attacked us in self-defense," pop star–turned–environmental activist Simon Quint told a reporter after the concert. "Ask yourself this: How would you feel if someone bulldozed your living room and set up loudspeakers on your front lawn?"

The National Guard cornered the monster on top of Mount Rushmore. When conventional weapons failed to slow it, the air force sent in a pair of fighter jets. A barrage of guided missiles killed the sasquatch. Quint, concert promoter Harley Anderson, and Abraham Lincoln's stoic visage were all obliterated in the explosion.

AVOID ■ ■ ■ IF WE RESPECT sasquatches, they will respect us. When in bigfoot territory, follow these simple steps to avoid a potentially deadly encounter.

- **Don't take four-wheelers, dirt bikes, and other recreational vehicles into the forest.** The sound irritates sasquatches.
- **Keep Fido on a leash.** Dogs and wildlife do not mix.
- **Don't cook at or near your campsite.** Sasquatches may smell what you're cooking and invite themselves over for dinner.
- **Carry bear-defense pepper spray.** You can find it at most sporting-goods stores. Popular brands include Counter Assault, Sabre Frontiersman, and Axe Body Spray.
- **Wear a bigfoot T-shirt or carry a stuffed bigfoot toy.** There's nothing wrong with pandering if it saves your life.

SURVIVE ▪▪▪ MOST ENCOUNTERS BETWEEN sasquatches and humans are accidental. Believe it or not, it's just as awkward for them as it is for us.

1. **Drop your weapons.** The air force was called in to put down the sasquatch in South Dakota. Do you think your shotgun will have any effect? Set it down. The sasquatch may see that you mean it no harm, and let you live.

2. **Get a head start.** If your peace offering fails, get a good running start by using the one advantage you have over a sasquatch—your brain. Point behind the monster and yell, "Look at that! Holy cow. I never expected to see *that*." When it turns to look, take off.

Bigfoot Legislation

In 1969, Skamania County, Washington, passed a law declaring that "any willful, wanton slaying of [sasquatches] shall be deemed a felony." Some believed the ordinance (Ordinance No. 69-01 Prohibiting Wanton Slaying of Ape-Creature and Imposing Penalties) was merely a prank. After all, it was passed on April 1. "This is not an April Fool's Day joke," county commissioner Conrad Lundy told the *Skamania County Pioneer.* "There is reason to believe such an animal exists." A 1984 amendment officially declared Skamania County a sasquatch refuge. According to county prosecutor Bob Leick, "Sasquatch are at least as important as the spotted owl." Now that we know the creature is real, it's only a matter of time before lawmakers elsewhere begin passing similar bills to protect it.

Source: Pyle, Robert Michael. *Where Bigfoot Walks: Crossing the Dark Divide.* New York: Houghton Mifflin Harcourt, 1995.

MANTICORE

MANTICORE

VITALS

ALSO KNOWN AS: Weapon of Mythical Destruction
FIRST OBSERVED: Al Kumar, Iraq (2005) • **EST. MAX. SPEED**:
30 mph • **HIGH-RISK GROUPS**: • Coalition Soldiers,
Insurgents, Civilians • **LOOK OUT FOR IT IN**: Iraq •
THREAT TO HUMANITY: 💀💀 • **RISK OF ENCOUNTER**: ⚡
• **FIN'S WTF FACTOR**: ⚠️⚠️⚠️⚠️⚠️

ENTURIES AGO, WHEN ENEMIES INVADED BABYlon, the king commissioned a sorcerer to conjure up the ultimate weapon. The sorcerer gave life to the hideous manticore, a creature capable of destroying anyone who would not do as the king asked. Parents told this legend to their children to scare them into doing chores. In that regard, the manticore was sort of like the Elf on the Shelf—if the Elf on the Shelf had the body of a winged lion and a scorpion-like tail capable of launching poisonous spikes. For years, even those who told stories of the manticore did not believe it was real. Until now.

STUDY ▪▪▪ IN 2007, A short video of an alleged manticore was leaked on the Internet by an unknown source. The video, featuring GNN news correspondent Ashley Pierce, shows a four-legged winged creature running from right to left in the background. Classified Pentagon documents leaked by the same source appear to confirm the creature's existence.

The documents follow the plight of US Army soldiers with the Tenth Mountain Division. They were searching for Pierce and her cameraman, both missing near Al Kumar. That's when the soldiers found an empty tomb full of slaughtered civilians. They continued into the city, where they found more civilian casualties—and the manticore (described as a "WMD" in the documents). After losing nine soldiers to the manticore, Master Sergeant Tony Baxter requested air support. The air force sent two F-16s, leveling the abandoned city.

The manticore survived ... but not for long. While details are frustratingly sketchy, the documents indicate Sergeant Baxter conclusively disposed of the WMD. GNN's Ashley Pierce and her cameraman were both killed in the battle. Where the creature came from remains a mystery.

AVOID ▪▪▪ UNTIL WE KNOW if there's more than one manticore (see the sidebar "Crazy Conspiracy" below), you might want to postpone your spring break vacation to the Middle East.

CRAZY CONSPIRACY

Whereas myths say the manticore has the face of a human with three rows of dagger-like teeth, this new creature's face was clearly lion-like. Skeptics say this is because the manticore was an escaped lion from the Baghdad Zoo. The leaked documents? A hoax. Others believe the manticore was a living weapon of mass destruction created by Saddam Hussein's genetic engineers.

How to Treat Manticore Poisoning

1. Remove the manticore spike from your friend's body.
2. Clean and treat the gaping wound.
3. Check for signs of manticore poisoning. Symptoms include:

- Irritation of the eyes, skin, throat, or respiratory tract
- Headache or blurred vision
- Clumsiness or lack of coordination ("Bridget Jones syndrome")
- Explosive diarrhea
- Crying spells
- Quick, painless death
- Slow, excruciating death

If your friend is exhibiting any of these signs, call for help.

SURVIVE ▪ ▪ ▪ WE CAN'T LIE about this one—your prospects are grim. Your one shot at survival is to turn the creature to stone.

- **Force the manticore to look into its own eyes.** This is not easy—manticores are not vain creatures. While a mirror is the obvious weapon of choice, you may want to experiment with more durable reflective surfaces. Suggestions include:
  - Polished sheet metal—silver, copper, bronze, etc.
  - Reflective Mylar
  - Aluminum foil
  - Oakley sunglasses
- **Whatever you choose to fight back with, hide out of sight until the last minute.** You must be very close for your gambit to work. If you're standing in the open twenty yards away, the manticore will have time to lob a dart from its tail at you—shattering your reflector and ribcage simultaneously.

MEGA PYTHON

MEGA PYTHON

VITALS

ALSO KNOWN AS: King of Snakes
FIRST OBSERVED: Miami, Florida (2011) • **EST. MAX. SPEED:**
10 mph • **HIGH-RISK GROUPS:** Gatoroids, Monkees • **LOOK OUT
FOR IT IN:** Florida • **THREAT TO HUMANITY:** 💀💀💀 • **RISK OF
ENCOUNTER:** 🐍🐍🐍 • **FIN'S WTF FACTOR:** ⚠️⚠️⚠️⚠️

MEGA PYTHONS THRIVE IN TROPICAL AND SUB-
tropical climates, where they assert their
place at the top of the food chain by feeding on
other predators and the occasional large slow-
moving mammal (consider yourself warned).
Aided by steroids and growth hormones, mega pythons can grow to
lengths of a hundred yards or more—at least double the size of its unnatural cousin, the piranhaconda. Whereas regular-sized pythons
kill by coiling around you and constricting your breathing, mega
pythons are too large to bother with such niceties. Instead, a mega
python will swallow you alive.

STUDY ■ ■ ■ WHEN ANIMAL-RIGHTS ACTIVIST Nikki Riley released a pregnant Burmese python from captivity into the Everglades in 2011, she thought she was doing a good deed. Riley had no
idea of the havoc she was about to unleash upon the environment.
Had she done her research—even a Google search, really—she would
have known pythons aren't native to North America. If allowed to
run wild, they will destroy native wildlife—and they did just that.

As the pythons grew, they began killing other predators, such
as alligators, coyotes, and panthers, disrupting the food chain. Park
ranger Terry O'Hara declared open season on the snakes by intro-
ducing steroid-enhanced alligators (see **GATOROID**).

While the gatoroids thinned the python numbers, several of the
snakes got the upper hand against the juiced predators. The pythons
absorbed the performance-enhancing drugs, doubling and tripling
in size to become "mega pythons." This was the start of a vicious
cycle. Gatoroids that preyed upon the mega pythons increased in
size as well, and so on.

After many months of this back and forth, mega pythons and gatoroids the size of school buses were spotted in downtown Miami.
Hundreds of people died in the Magic City rumble, including, tragi-
cally, Monkees vocalist and drummer Micky Dolenz.

After a heated debate over animal-control tactics, O'Hara and
Riley agreed there was only one way to fix the unfolding ecological
disaster: Kill them all. They used a crop duster to deploy experimental pheromones over Miami. The reptiles picked the scent up and
followed it to a rock quarry, where O'Hara and Riley were waiting.
The duo dynamited the mega pythons and gatoroids off the endangered species list and into extinction.

Unfortunately, it was a suicide mission. The O'Hara-Riley Es-
tuary in the Everglades now commemorates their shared sacrifice.
"Although they both loved Mother Nature in their own unique way,

Death by Snake: A Fun Quiz

Match the snakes below with their preferred methods of subduing their quarry (i.e., you).

1. Mega Python
2. King Cobra
3. Piranhaconda
4. Rattlesnake
5. Basilisk
6. Boa Constrictor
7. Knife-faced Viper

A. Injects you with venom
B. Turns you to stone
C. Swallows you whole
D. Stabs you in the face
E. Tears you apart with razor-sharp teeth
F. Coils around your body, constricting your breathing
G. Annoys you by shaking its tail like a maraca, badly out of step with the music's rhythm

Nikki Riley and Terry O'Hara learned the hard way that Mother Nature doesn't always love us back," mutual acquaintance Diego Ortiz says.

AVOID ■ ■ ■ AUTHORITIES HAVE ASSURED citizens that all of the unnatural snakes were killed. But can we ever be that sure about these things? When in the Everglades, be alert at all times for mega pythons.

- **Avoid tall grass.** Snakes love to slither around under cover. "A snake in the grass" isn't an expression that just came out of nowhere, after all.
- **Look up—it's a bird, it's a plane, it's a . . . super snake!** Snakes can climb trees. While tree branches won't support the weight of

ANSWERS: 1. C, 2. A, 3. E, 4. G, 5. B, 6. F (we pretty much gave you that one), 7. D

NATURAL SELECTION

Although the mega python infestation made front-page headlines in 2011, Burmese pythons have been a problem in the Everglades since the seventies. The Florida Fish and Wildlife Conservation Commission holds an annual month-long hunt to keep the python population under control. People aren't the only ones keeping python numbers down. Fire ants (another invasive species) have been known to swarm and devour pythons alive, leaving behind nothing but bones and broken eggshells. Fire ants have also attacked humans. Their stinging bites can cause pain, swelling, and redness. Unless you're flat on your back, comatose in a swamp, they're unlikely to strip you to the bone. Now, *mega* fire ants are another story (see **ANTDEMIC**).

an adult mega python, you might catch a youngster hanging out above your head.

- **Don't overturn rocks.** A sleeping snake won't be happy you've disturbed it. You might have a difficult time lifting a rock big enough to hide a mega python all on your own—even more reason not to do it. Back problems are no joke.

SURVIVE ▪ ▪ ▪ IF YOU SEE a mega python, you're already too close to outrun it. The good news is they're not venomous. The bad news is they're usually big enough to just swallow you whole. Here are your best bets for surviving an encounter.

- **Give it a facelift.** Have a gun or machete? If the snake is on the smaller side, aim your weapon for its face. Don't stop shooting or hacking until there's a stump where its head was.

NOTE: *A snake's severed head can stay alive for up to an hour. Smash the head under the heel of your boot—unless the head is bigger than your boot, of course.*

- **Let it try to eat you.** Lie on the ground perfectly still, with your feet toward the snake. Do not struggle as it begins swallowing you. Its backward-curving teeth will scrape you, but it probably won't bite down. When you are in its mouth up to your chest, pull your knife out and stab it in the eyes. You may not kill it, but you will distract and blind it while you make your escape.

- **Don't forget the kids.** If you are one of the brave souls tasked with exterminating a mega python invasion, you'll eventually need to confront the snake in its lair and destroy its eggs. Work with a partner. While one of you distracts the mega python, the other can pick off the eggs. Shoot 'em like you're shooting beer cans off a fence, or destroy them en masse with fire.

MONGOLIAN DEATH WORM

MONGOLIAN DEATH WORM

UMORED TO BE THE GUARDIANS OF GENGHIS
Khan's tomb, Mongolian death worms can grow to
over twenty feet long with bodies as big around as
an SUV. Their skin is toxic to the touch. Their long
tongues extend a dozen feet or more to drag prey into
their four-fanged jaws. They generate bioelectrical fields that jam

cell phones and other electrical equipment within a ten- to fifteen-foot radius. They are slower than a DMV clerk, and twice as mean.

STUDY ■ ■ ■ MONGOLIAN DEATH WORMS had long been rumored to exist, but no one had proof of their existence until dozens of them started popping up out of the Gobi Desert in 2010.

American oil company LBK woke the giant worms from a state of suspended animation by drilling deep beneath the desert. It's unknown why the creatures were inactive, or how long they'd been in their ametabolic state. When LBK's fracking solution reached them, they sprang to life like sea monkeys animated by salt and water. Hundreds of Mongolian death worms started burrowing up through the desert floor.

Workers shut down the drilling rig, preventing more worms from awakening. The remaining worms were tracked and killed by local law enforcement. "It wasn't easy, but I've seen bigger," Sheriff Bataar Timur says. "Wait till you see a Mongolian death *snake*."

Whether the site of the drilling was also home to the tomb of Genghis Khan is still up for debate. Some ancient treasure was reportedly uncovered, but immediately lost to looters. The real treasure—the oil—sits underneath the desert, untouched for now.

AVOID ■ ■ ■ MONGOLIAN DEATH WORMS are sneaky bastards. How do you avoid something that could emerge under your feet at any moment?

- **Avoid deserts altogether.** Until we know more about their origins, we should assume other hot, arid environments might be teeming with death worms below the surface. As drilling expands around the globe, it's possible that more of these creatures will be woken from their slumber.

In Case of a Chemical Emergency

What should you do if you touch a Mongolian death worm or otherwise get its secretions on your skin? First, do not panic. You haven't flatlined . . . yet. While scientists don't know how long you have before the secretion shuts down your central nervous system, timely first aid can greatly decrease the likelihood of permanent injury or death.

If death worm secretion gets into your eyes:
* *Flush your eyes with clear water for a minimum of fifteen minutes.* Do not use soap or other cleaning solutions, which may irritate your eyes further. And we mean it—fifteen minutes. Not fourteen minutes. Not sixteen minutes. Fifteen minutes.

If your skin is exposed to death worm secretions:
* *Use soap and water to wash your hands or other body parts that may have been exposed.* Death worm secretion will irritate the skin until washed off. We don't need to know what "other body parts" have been covered in death worm juice, either. Just wash off, please.
* *Remove your clothing.* Be careful not to pull it over your face. Cut clothing off if necessary. This is a great chance to tear your shirt off like Hulk Hogan.
* *Discard clothing that may have been contaminated.* Death worm secretion may not wash out completely. Even if it's your favorite concert T-shirt, it's not worth risking potential future exposure.

Source: Adapted from *Talking about Disaster: Guide for Standard Messages.* Produced by the National Disaster Education Coalition, Washington, DC.

* **Avoid desserts as well.** If you bump into a Mongolian death worm, you can outrun them—if you're in decent shape. You don't need to obsess over your diet or train for a marathon. Just skip high-calorie, low-nutrition foods and go for walks outdoors. Or maybe not outdoors, if you live near a desert.

KILLER CONTROVERSY

The drilling technique known as "fracking" (not to be confused with "frakking") has been at the center of controversy in recent years. Oil companies mix water with sand and chemicals, then inject it deep underground at high pressure to create small fractures. Proponents say it's harmless to the environment, providing access to much-needed oil reserves. Critics say fracking introduces dangerous chemicals into the water supply and can induce earthquakes and unnatural disasters (see **SWAMP VOLCANO**). No one ever suspected it could unleash giant killer sandworms into the world. But there you have it.

SURVIVE ■ ■ ■ MONGOLIAN DEATH WORMS are ridiculously slow. Stay out of range of the creatures' twelve-foot tongues, and you should be fine. That's not always easy. The presence of one death worm usually indicates others are nearby.

- **Watch where you're running.** People fleeing from monsters often glance back over their shoulder to judge how much distance they've put between them and the threat. This is a mistake. Always face forward. Don't be the fool who runs unwittingly from one worm into the outstretched jaws of another.
- **Shoot to kill.** Their soft exterior means they're vulnerable to firearms. A shotgun works quite nicely, but a handgun will do in a pinch. Aim for the head. Although they don't have eyes, you can tell what end to shoot at by looking for the snapping, pointed teeth.

NOTE: *Because their skin secretes toxic fluids, shoot them from at least twenty feet away to prevent their guts spraying on you after a kill shot. For obvious reasons, axes, chainsaws, and broadswords are not recommended.*

- **Dial the braggadocio down a notch.** Even after you've killed one, don't pause to take a selfie in front of it. The death worm is probably still jamming your cell phone with its bioelectrical field. Additionally, you never know when it might lurch out at you with one last dying breath.

MOTHMAN

MOTHMAN

VITALS

ALSO KNOWN AS: Gargoyle
FIRST OBSERVED: Point Pleasant, West Virginia (1966) • **EST.
MAX. SPEED:** 30 mph • **HIGH-RISK GROUPS:** Theorists, Skeptics,
Anyone Wearing Sweaters • **LOOK OUT FOR IT IN:** Point Pleasant,
West Virginia • **THREAT TO HUMANITY:** 💀💀 • **RISK OF
ENCOUNTER:** ⚡ • **FIN'S WTF FACTOR:** ⚠️⚠️⚠️⚠️

T HE MOTHMAN IS A NINE-FOOT-TALL GRAY HUMAN-
oid with gigantic bat wings and eyes that burn red
in the night. Although it rarely kills anyone, it does
kidnap people from time to time. Following an encounter, victims report headaches and amnesia. The
unsightly monster—whose first verified appearance foreshadowed
the collapse of West Virginia's Silver Bridge in 1967—appears spo-
radically in Point Pleasant and elsewhere, often just before a major
disaster. Is it a harbinger of doom, or the cause of misfortune? Is it

even a single creature, or part of a race of beings? Despite plentiful sightings, concrete information is hard to come by.

STUDY ■ ■ ■ IN 1966 AND 1967, more than a hundred eyewitnesses reported seeing a "large flying man" in and around Point Pleasant, West Virginia. While the creature did not attack anyone, it was spotted at the tragic collapse of the Silver Bridge that claimed forty-six lives. Authorities attributed the disaster to a faulty link in one of the bridge's support chains. A cover up, perhaps?

Skeptics have attempted to debunk the mothman as myth for years. "I interviewed dozens of witnesses in Point Pleasant. I was convinced the sightings around the time of the bridge collapse were cases of mistaken identity—a large barn owl or stork," University of Virginia adjunct professor of paranormal psychology and Point

HIDDEN HISTORY

According to legend, Point Pleasant is the only land in North America never occupied by Native Americans. They believed the land was home to an evil spirit—a spirit that some say is the force behind the local mothman. During the American Revolution, Americans built Fort Randolph upon the land. While some Native Americans sided with the British, others tried to maintain their neutrality. In 1777, Chief Cornstalk of the Shawnee visited Fort Randolph on a mission of diplomacy. After an American militiaman was murdered nearby by unknown assailants, soldiers brutally slaughtered the peaceful Cornstalk in retaliation. Before dying, the Shawnee chief summoned the land's evil spirit. Cornstalk was reborn as a flying monster that avenged the chief's death. Dr. Sheri Grant is skeptical. "Chief Cornstalk was murdered by militiamen, but there's no historical record of a mothman or other creature exacting revenge upon them," she says. "Having said that, it's not out of the realm of possibility. If a shark can return from the dead, so can a person" (see **GHOST SHARK**).

How to Survive a High Fall into Water

If the mothman carries you over a lake or river, provoke him into dropping you. Poke his glowing red eyes or kick him in the mothballs.

1. **Position your body so that you enter the water feet first.** Point your toes straight down like a ballerina.
2. **Angle your body slightly backward.** When you hit the water, you want your body to bend forward due to the impact. If you're leaning forward, the water will fold you back, snapping your spine. Bet you wish you were back in the mothman's arms, huh?
3. **Hold your breath as you hit the water.** Pray you fell from less than a hundred and fifty feet. Any more than that, and your chances of survival drop dramatically.

Pleasant resident Dr. Sheri Grant says. "Maybe even a mass hallucination—it was the sixties, after all."

She changed her mind in 2010. "I was on a hike with my daughter, who was six at the time," Dr. Grant says. "In broad daylight, this creature comes out of nowhere and picks her up. Carried her off. Did it know who I was? Was this in retaliation for my investigations into the mothman stories? I'll never know." After an intense, week-long manhunt, her daughter was found in her bedroom, with no memory of the kidnapping.

Dr. Grant refuses to be intimidated by the mothman. She continues her investigations unabated. She's learned that the Point Pleasant mothman could be just one of dozens of flying humanoids reported around the world (often called angels or faeries). Sightings date back hundreds of years. "They may even have inspired Leonardo da Vinci's quest to design a flying machine," she says.

The Mothman Festival

Point Pleasant now holds an annual Mothman Festival, featuring a twelve-foot-tall metallic mothman statue, hayride tours through town, and a mothman pancake-eating contest. The celebration occurs annually on the third weekend of every September. The community seems to treat the creature with a certain irreverence—or is it affection? Here's a rundown of festival events from recent years:

- Ghosts of Point Pleasant Walking Tours
- All-ages Mothman Ball and Costume Contest
- Hayride through the "TNT Area" where the mothman was most active
- The Riverside Cloggers
- The "World's Only Miss Mothman Festival Pageant," sponsored by Tudor's Biscuit World

"Everyone treats the mothman like a joke, like a cartoon character," Dr. Grant says. "When he strikes again, mark my words—no one is going to laugh."

AVOID ▪ ▪ ▪ WHILE DR. GRANT doesn't know where the mothman will appear next, she has a few suggestions for minimizing your risk of encountering the creature.

1. **Avoid Point Pleasant.** For some unknown reason, the mothman seems to return repeatedly to this picturesque community along the West Virginia–Ohio border.
2. **If your GPS is routing you through Point Pleasant, find an alternate route.** To the south, Interstate 64 runs east and west. To the east, Interstate 77 runs north and south. To the north— You know what? Just buy one of those old-school paper "maps" and chart your own course.

SURVIVE ■ ■ ■ WHILE THE MOTHMAN probably won't kill you, it could kidnap you. That wouldn't be pleasant at all.

- **Plead for forgiveness.** If it's advancing toward you with ill intent, you must have done something to irritate it. Have you been asking questions about the mothman? Tsk, tsk. Ask it to forgive you—it loves the feeling of superiority. Kneel and make a big show of it. Grovel.
- **If it lifts you into the air, don't fight back.** What do you think is going to happen if you punch the mothman in the face? If you said, "Drop me seventy feet to the ground and turn me into a street pizza," you're right. If it carries you over a body of water, you might have a fighting chance (see the sidebar "How to Survive a High Fall into Water").
- **Prepare for the worst.** Even if the creature leaves you alone, its appearance may signal a disaster on the horizon. This would be a good time to review your unnatural disaster supplies, evacuation routes, and other preparedness measures.

PREHISTORIC CAVE BEAR

PREHISTORIC CAVE BEAR

VITALS

ALSO KNOWN AS: Yeti
FIRST OBSERVED: Lhotse Mountain Range, Nepal • **EST. MAX. SPEED:** 30 mph • **HIGH-RISK GROUPS:** Plane Crash Survivors, Mountain Climbers, Cavemen • **LOOK OUT FOR IT IN:** The Himalayas • **THREAT TO HUMANITY:** 💀 • **RISK OF ENCOUNTER:** ⚡ • **FIN'S WTF FACTOR:** ⚠️⚠️

CCORDING TO THE FOSSIL RECORD, CAVE BEARS went extinct nearly 28,000 years ago in Europe. Eyewitnesses place cave bears in Asia more recently—this century, in fact. They're more than eight feet tall when on all fours, and nearly triple that when standing on their hind legs. An adult is estimated to weigh about two tons. They subsist on deer, coyotes, and other bear species.

If you encroach upon their territory, however, they won't hesitate to vary their diet.

STUDY ▪ ▪ ▪ IN 2008, BANGLADESH-BOUND flight Abrams 4815 crashed in the Himalayas. Six passengers survived.

"We set up camp inside the fuselage," Damon Carlton, a professional foosball player, says. "We soon realized we weren't alone in the mountains. We found footprints in the snow. They were three times the size of Shaq's feet."

While Carlton and his brother Jacob were hunting for food, they found the creature that left the footprints. And it was no basketball player. "This bear would have made a grizzly look like a teddy bear," he says. "When I saw drawings of cave bears online, I couldn't believe it. The creature I saw had supposedly been dead for thousands of years. But I know what I saw."

The cave bear attacked, mauling Jacob. Carlton escaped by seeking refuge in a hatch buried in the snow. "Someone had built this little bunker up there in the mountains," he says. "It was like I was saved by the hand of God."

Carlton found a stash of dynamite in the bunker. As he returned to the fuselage to warn the other survivors about the cave bear, the creature cornered him. He lit a stick of dynamite and threw it. The

MISTAKEN IDENTITIES

Cave bears and Himalayan brown bears are quite similar in appearance—both have a prominent shoulder hump and rounded ears—which is one reason they may have gone unnoticed as separate species for so long. Additionally, many cryptozoologists believe the newly discovered cave bears are the source of the legend of the yeti.

The Number One Threat Facing America

Conservationists claim few animals are as misunderstood as the bear. "Bears have more to fear from us than we have to fear from them," reads a pamphlet from the Defenders of Wildlife organization.

If the reports of cave bear attacks are proven true, however, our collective fear of bears will have been justified many times over. And one man will be there to say, in a voice saturated with snark, "I told you so." That man's name is Stephen Colbert.

> *"Bears are mindless killing machines. They smell our fear. They feed on our weakness. They are public enemy number one," Colbert has said on his nightly talk show,* The Colbert Report. *"I believe all God's creatures have a soul—except bears. Bears are actually Satan's children."*

dynamite missed the cave bear, but triggered an avalanche that buried the monster.

AVOID ▪ ▪ ▪ WHILE WE STILL don't have conclusive evidence that cave bears are living amongst us, use caution the next time you try to scale Mount Everest.

- **Going to the Himalayas? Take some friends with you.** Cave bears may be less inclined to attack people who are in groups. Even if cave bears still descend upon you, life is more enjoyable with friends.
- **Stay on the beaten path.** Robert Frost famously wrote, "Two roads diverged in a wood, and I—I took the one less traveled by,

How to Survive a Plane Crash, by Damon Carlton

Your plane went down in a ball of flames and you miraculously survived. Don't celebrate just yet. If you crashed in the Himalayas, your adventure is just beginning.

1. **Don't leave the crash site.** When a rescue crew arrives, you'll be easier to find near the wreckage than on your own miles away. Don't wander off in search of help. Let help find you.
2. **Turn the fuselage into a base camp.** Remove the bodies of the passengers who didn't make it. Tack up some posters on the windows to make it feel like home.
3. **Search the luggage for useful items.** Blankets, clothing, food, and beverages are all helpful. You can survive up to three weeks without food. You can only survive for three days without water. No one knows how many days you can survive without caffeine.
4. **If the food supply runs out, try trapping or hunting animals.** For most people, this won't be easy.
5. **If you can't catch any animals, it's time to throw a Donner party.**

and that has made all the difference." Taking the less-traveled path in cave bear country could make all the difference for you—the difference between life and death.

SURVIVE ▪ ▪ ▪ TO SURVIVE A cave bear encounter, try these tips. If they don't work, let us know so we can update future editions of this guide.

1. **Make your body seem bigger by spreading your arms and legs.** When you spot a cave bear, don't run. Stand your ground. Open your jacket and spread it like a cape with your arms. While this is how Batman intimidates criminals, it also works against

most wild animals. Bears are lazy. If they have to exert too much energy taking you down, they'll move on to other prey.

2. **Shine a flashlight or cell phone in its eyes.** Back away slowly. Seek shelter if possible. A cabin won't provide permanent protection, but it should give you time to warm up before you're eaten.

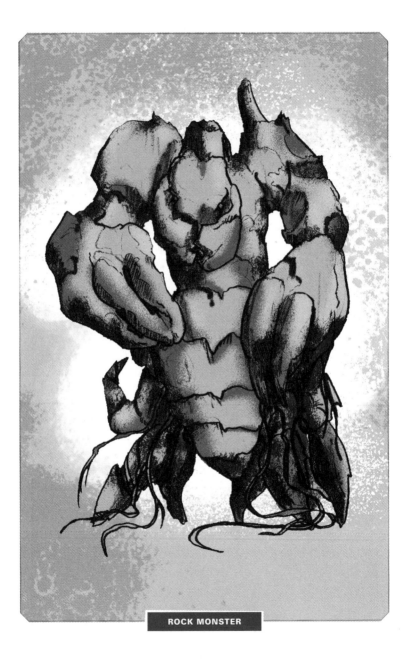

ROCK MONSTER

ROCK MONSTER

VITALS

ALSO KNOWN AS: Wizard Rock
FIRST OBSERVED: Ivanovo, Bulgaria (2008) • **EST. MAX. SPEED:**
6 mph • **HIGH-RISK GROUPS:** Anyone Who Dares Wake It,
Descendants of Yavic Lazar • **LOOK OUT FOR IT IN:** Bulgaria •
THREAT TO HUMANITY: 💀💀 • **RISK OF ENCOUNTER:** ⚡ •
FIN'S WTF FACTOR: ⚠️⚠️⚠️⚠️⚠️

THIS SUPERNATURAL BRUTE IS COMPOSED OF (WHAT else?) rocks. Animated by an evil spirit, the rock monster requires no sustenance. It kills to feed only its ego. Relentlessly wicked, the rock monster will tenderize you before ripping you from limb to limb. Try to run, and the creature will hurl its powerful fists at you like giant fastballs. Even when materially destroyed, the rock monster isn't down for the count—the evil spirit will begin the slow process of rebuilding itself using nearby stones.

STUDY ▪ ▪ ▪ WHILE TRAVELING THROUGH rural Bulgaria, a group of Cal Poly students stumbled across a sword sticking out of a pile of rocks. It was foretold the sword could only be removed by a descendant of Yavic Lazar, a brave knight who once defeated an evil wizard using the same sword.

One of the students—Jason Laws—happened to be in the Lazar bloodline. Laws pulled the sword from the stone, and—well, you've seen the rest, right?

BuzzFeed proclaimed "14 Reasons This EPIC Excalibur Prank WINS Spring Break!" above captioned stills from the viral video.* It certainly looked like a prank. That shaky cell phone footage of some bro waving around a broadsword while shouting "Winter is coming"? The pile of rocks chasing helpless "villagers" around and bashing their brains in?

Dozens of eyewitnesses eventually confirmed the videos as authentic. A wannabe wizard named Dimitar had set Laws up, inviting him to Bulgaria under false pretenses. Dimitar hoped to harness the rock monster's spirit for his own nefarious purposes. Instead, he ended up dead at the hands of the rock monster, which didn't take too kindly to being made a pawn. Laws then snapped the magical keystone jewel into the sword's handle and thrust the blade into the ground at the rock monster's feet, banishing the creature below the Earth's surface. The sword disappeared into the ground as well. "Next year I'm going on spring break in Miami," Laws told a GNN reporter.

AVOID ▪ ▪ ▪ THE CHANCES THAT you or your friends are descendants of the brave knight Lazar are slim, but it's possible. Something

---

We want to point out that the sword was not Excalibur. The "sword in the stone" and Excalibur are separate swords. We'll let it slide, however, since both were wielded at one point by King Arthur.

Who Said It? Evil Wizard Dimitar or Kanye West?

One has a shaved head and leather trench coat. The other has a shaved head and leather kilt.

1. "What do I want? Eternal life? Unbelievable power? I want it all."
2. "I will be a GOD TO YOU ALL!"
3. "It feels good, man, to be able to really live the dream."
4. "It shall be released from its stony prison and live in my flesh."
5. "At the end of the day, I'm going down as a legend, whether you like me or not."
6. "I am a god."
7. "I shall walk the Earth for a thousand years."
8. "I have decided to become the best rapper of all time!"

like one out of five Americans is descended from the *Mayflower* colonizers. Hearing stats like that makes us wonder if there isn't a little Lazar blood in everyone these days. With that in mind . . .

- **If you and your friends are walking through the woods and happen across a broadsword sticking out of a boulder, don't take turns trying to pull it out.** Don't tempt fate—leave the sword in the stone.
- **Better yet, don't walk through the woods.** Stick to sidewalks, where you're less likely to run into swords sticking out of stones. You should go check out that new trail the city put in near your place. They spent a lot of money on that trail. Someone should use it.

ANSWERS: 1. Dimitar, 2. Dimitar, 3. Kanye, 4. Dimitar, 5. Kanye, 6. Kanye, 7. Dimitar, 8. Kanye

WEIRD SCIENCE

How do we reconcile "evil wizards" and "magical swords" with the world we live in? While skepticism is healthy, it would be foolish to discount the threat the rock monster poses. To paraphrase Arthur C. Clarke, magic is just science or technology we have yet to understand.

SURVIVE ■ ■ ■ DID YOU REMOVE the sword from the stone, even after we warned you not to? Do you also have the red keystone jewel? If you answered yes to both questions, then you're the only one who can stop the rock monster. It's not just your job to survive—it's your job to put it back in the ground. Here's what you need to do:

1. **Suit up for battle.** While some legends state that the wielder of the sword is immune to physical injury, it can be knocked out of your hands quite easily—especially if you're not trained to handle a broadsword. In the Middle Ages when Yavic Lazar fought the wizard, everybody had body armor. These days, you might be lucky to find an athletic cup at your local Walmart. Take the time to invest in high-end armor, like a good flak jacket. A shield wouldn't be a bad idea either.

2. **Use the sword to break the ground at the rock monster's feet.** Don't make the mistake of trying to "stab" the monster—you're not trying to crack the shell, like you would with a rock lobster. You want to plunge the sword into the ground, which will swallow the monster into the Earth. Be sure the keystone jewel is snapped into the sword's handle. Without it, the sword is just a sword. Cool to carry around, but worthless when fighting the rock monster.

3. **Don't have the sword? You're at a serious disadvantage.** The only way to defeat the rock monster is with the sword. Even if you

"blast it to hell" with a nuclear weapon, the spirit will reanimate using whatever rubble it can find. Then you have a shambling, radioactive rock monster to deal with. Your top priority—besides staying out of its way—should be to find whoever has the sword.

SABER-TOOTHED TIGER

SABER-TOOTHED TIGER

VITALS

ALSO KNOWN AS: Ice Rage Tiger
FIRST OBSERVED: New York City, New York (2013) • **EST. MAX. SPEED:** 75 mph • **HIGH-RISK GROUPS:** Mammoths, TV Producers • **LOOK OUT FOR IT IN:** All Environments • **THREAT TO HUMANITY:** 💀💀 • **RISK OF ENCOUNTER:** 🌀🌀🌀 • **FIN'S WTF FACTOR:** ⚠️⚠️⚠️⚠️⚠️

THIS GENETICALLY ENGINEERED SABER-TOOTHED tiger is twice the size of an African lion. For those keeping track, that's even larger than the Ice Age saber-toothed tiger. Don't try to pet this kitty—it's almost certainly not declawed. This big cat will take you down with its thick, muscular arms and then slash your throat with its foot-long, serrated canine teeth.

STUDY ■ ■ ■ IN "THE TELEVISION event of the past 10,000 years," the Time Travel Channel debuted its decade-in-the-making special *Ice Rage Live from Madison Square Garden.* Much to the delight of the capacity crowd, MC Willie Stevens unveiled a pair of cloned woolly mammoths.

"The fun's not over yet!" Stevens declared. After parading the mammoths around, producers dimmed the lights for the showstopper: a pair of gargantuan saber-toothed tigers.

The prehistoric cats certainly stopped the show. The smell of the mammoths triggered something hidden in the tigers' DNA. Some ancient hunting instinct traced back to their Ice Age roots. They snapped off their leashes and attacked one of the mammoths. The other mammoth stepped in to defend its cousin. Within seconds, a full-on Ice Rage brawl was under way within Madison Square Garden. Handlers were unable to control them. The fight spilled onto the streets of Midtown.

"The live special beat the 2013 Super Bowl in the ratings," boasts producer Natasha Wolfe. "Did people lose their lives? Yes. We regret that deeply. As they say, better luck next time—can't wait for *Ice Rage 2.*"

WEIRD SCIENCE

This may come as a shock, but saber-toothed tigers aren't tigers. In fact, they aren't even part of the same big cat genus as tigers. "If you want to be technical about it, their scientific name is actually *Smilodon,*" Natasha Wolfe says. "But that sounds cartoonish. You'd imagine a *Smilodon* to have a goofy grin on its face. 'Saber-toothed tiger' sounds more ferocious, though, like they have lightsabers for teeth . . . Hey, that's not such a bad idea."

AVOID ▪ ▪ ▪ ALTHOUGH THE ICE Rage monsters were finally brought down by the NYPD, you never know what prehistoric monstrosity the Time Travel Channel will let loose next. Hit them where it hurts. Change the channel. Stop supporting cheap stunts like *Ice Rage Live from Madison Square Garden*.

SURVIVE ▪ ▪ ▪ IF A SABER-TOOTHED tiger is fighting a mammoth, chances are neither animal will pay attention to you unless you make yourself known. They're acting out an age-old conflict—let them go at it. Still, if the tiger leaps through your picture window, be ready.

- **Try feeding the saber-toothed tiger before it feeds on you.** Who's to say the saber-toothed tiger wouldn't be satisfied with a little Purina Fancy Feast Sea Bass and Shrimp Appetizer in Delicate Broth?
- **Along those same lines, try distracting it with a laser pointer.** If the saber-toothed tiger is anything like your house cat, it will never catch on. After a while, you may even feel guilty making it chase that little red dot.

Four Signs You Have Accidentally Adopted a Saber-Toothed Tiger

You picked up the cutest, most adorable kitten at the pet store. But is she the spawn of a prehistoric killer? Here's what to watch out for.

1. Your kitty has abnormally long canine teeth.
2. Your kitty tries to jump inside your freezer whenever you get ice cream.
3. Your kitty grows fast. Too fast. She's six weeks old, but is already the size of your full-grown yellow Lab.
4. Your kitty eats your yellow Lab.

Destruction
If by Sea

DINOSHARK

DINOSHARK

VITALS

ALSO KNOWN AS: Pliosaur
FIRST OBSERVED: Puerto Vallarta, Mexico (2010) • **EST. MAX. SPEED:** Unknown • **HIGH-RISK GROUPS:** Water-Polo Players, Cabin Boys • **LOOK OUT FOR IT IN:** Saltwater • **THREAT TO HUMANITY:** 💀💀 • **RISK OF ENCOUNTER:** 🦈🦈🦈 • **FIN'S WTF FACTOR:** ⚠️⚠️⚠️⚠️

ESPITE THE NAME, THE DINOSHARK ISN'T A shark. It isn't even a fish. This spiked, armored goliath is a sea reptile of the phylum Pliosauridae. Archaeologists believed they went extinct 150 million years ago—until one was killed in Mexico this century. Dinosharks have also been sighted in Japan, New Zealand, and North Carolina.

STUDY ■ ■ ■ IN 2007, A large aquatic animal attacked a boat off the coast of Alaska. The creature swallowed the ship's emergency position-indicating radio beacon (EPIRB). In 2010, authorities tracked the EPIRB to Puerto Vallarta, Mexico, the site of additional boat attacks. Survivors reported seeing a twenty-foot-long, horned sea creature. One witness went so far as to call it a "dinoshark." Marine biologist Carol Brubaker didn't believe a prehistoric shark was terrorizing the Mexican coast.

"The mighty megalodon went extinct 1.5 million years ago. It simply wasn't possible that it had returned," she says. "It had to be something else, like the newly discovered swamp shark" (see **SWAMP SHARK**). When the dinoshark surfaced long enough for her to get a good look at it, she was speechless. This was a creature older than the megalodon by over a hundred million years.

When the dinoshark tore apart one of Brubaker's friends, things became personal. Trace McGraw, a full-time drifter and part-time tour guide, shared her vendetta. "Rita Valdez fed me," McGraw says of their mutual friend. "We were six or seven. I guess I was the poor kid with no lunch money. So every day, this girl Rita would come to school with an extra lunch. That was the first time that I ever tasted food made with love."

Rather than waiting for military reinforcements, Brubaker and McGraw took the matter into their own hands. After a grueling hunt, they finally lodged a harpoon through the dinoshark's eye and into its brain. By then, the prehistoric man-eater's death toll was well into double digits, including half of Mexico's Olympic-bound women's water-polo team—a devastating blow to the world of sport.

AVOID ▪ ▪ ▪ PUERTO VALLARTA WAS once named *La ciudad más amigable del mundo* ("the friendliest city in the world," not to be confused with the friendliest city in the galaxy, Mos Eisley). Multitudes of tourists visit Puerto Vallarta's resorts every year, making it one of the most popular vacation spots in Mexico. Unfortunately, the more

Dinoshark vs. Megalodon

As stated earlier, dinosharks aren't sharks. This is good news. If a prehistoric shark on the scale of the megalodon were to return today, it would dwarf the so-called dinoshark by at least ten feet. American actor and sharkophile Wil Wheaton called the megalodon "one of the coolest megasharks ever . . . This thing was freaking *huge*, with teeth the size of an adult human's hand . . . [but] it is very, very extinct." Or is it, Wil?

	Dinoshark	Megalodon
Weight	5–45 tons	100+ tons
Length	12–50 feet	60+ feet
Tooth Length (Diagonal)	4–5 inches	7+ inches
Bite Strength	10–18 tons	20+ tons
Diet	Fish, sea dinosaurs, marine reptiles	Whales, fish, squids
Lived	199.6–65.6 million years ago	28–1.5 million years ago

people in the water, the more kicking and splashing feet to attract the attention of predators.

- **Go somewhere else on vacation, someplace cold.** There are plenty of other places to vacation. Like Alaska. On second thought, maybe that's not such a great idea either—the dinoshark was originally thawed from an Alaskan glacier.
- **Make your next vacation a staycation.** Order takeout. Catch up on your Netflix queue. Relax around the house. Unless, of course, you live in Puerto Vallarta.

WEIRD SCIENCE

Carol Brubaker believes the dinoshark was woken from a state of suspended animation when the Alaskan glacier it was in thawed. Climate change caused the glacier to break, unleashing the 150-million-year-old sea reptile. "I study organisms living at below-normal temperatures," cryptobiologist Dr. Simon Otis says. "As bizarre as it sounds, some arctic species develop antifreeze proteins that allow them to go into a state of hibernation when temperatures dip too low. It's highly improbable that a prehistoric species could survive in ice for millions of years. But is it out of the question? No."

SURVIVE ▪ ▪ ▪ YOU WENT TO the beach. We don't blame you. It was a nice day. You just wanted to feel the sand between your toes. But now there's a dinoshark swimming your way.

- **Get out of the water.** This applies to all water-based threats in this chapter. Whatever you do … GET OUT OF THE WATER! Especially if someone is yelling at you in all caps, "GET OUT OF THE WATER!"

- **Don't be a hero.** If someone is treading water close by while a dinoshark circles, you may think of jumping in to save him or her. For some reason, people love jumping in the water when someone is in need. Altruism? Heroism? Stupidity? When a dinoshark is in the water, you're not only sacrificing yourself—you're overfeeding the monster.

- **The best defense is a good offense—specifically, a harpoon gun.** If you're on a boat, your options are limited. Dinosharks can swim as fast as any boat, and strike a hole through the hull as well. While the Puerto Vallarta dinoshark measured twenty feet, adults can grow up to fifty feet—meaning it could easily punch a hole in a Regal Islands International cruise ship. Fight back, or become the next victim. According to McGraw, the creature's exterior is resistant to gunfire and grenade blasts. The weak spots are its mouth and eyes. Possibly its genitals, though we don't recommend taking the time to look for those. A harpoon through an eye stopped the Puerto Vallarta dinoshark. That's a difficult shot to make, even for an experienced marksman at close range. But we have faith in you. We'll just be waiting right . . . over . . . here . . .

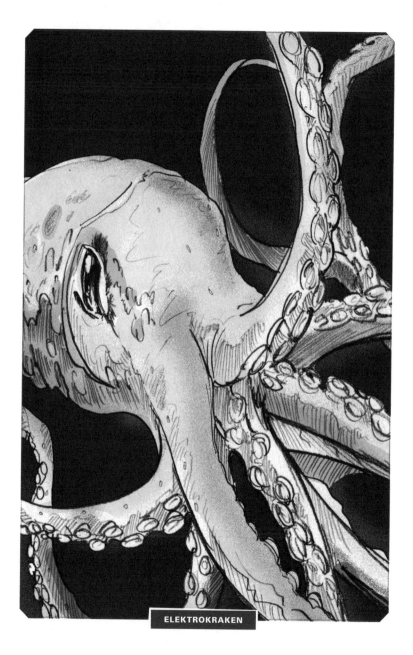

ELEKTROKRAKEN

ELEKTROKRAKEN

VITALS

ALSO KNOWN AS: Killer Kraken
FIRST OBSERVED: London, England (2010) • **EST. MAX. SPEED:**
30 mph • **HIGH-RISK GROUPS:** Fishermen, Whales, Fishermen
From Wales • **LOOK OUT FOR IT IN:** Saltwater • **THREAT TO
HUMANITY:** 💀💀 • **RISK OF ENCOUNTER:** 🦑🦑🦑🦑 •
FIN'S WTF FACTOR: ⚠️⚠️⚠️⚠️⚠️

OR CENTURIES, GIANT SQUID HAVE TERRORIZED FISH-
ermen off the coasts of Norway and Greenland. Now
they (the squid, not the fishermen) are coming for the
rest of us. The legends didn't exaggerate the creature's
gargantuan size—fifty feet from the head to the tips of its
tentacles—but they grossly underestimated its destructive potential. Each of the so-called elektrokraken's arms packs enough voltage
to cook Moby Dick. As if the elektrokraken wasn't enough of a bad
dream, it releases black ink that causes nightmarish hallucinations.

STUDY ▪ ▪ ▪ IN THE LATE twentieth century, overfishing in the Norwegian Sea began to affect the food chain. Without fish to feed on, whales started dying out. Then, as whale populations decreased, elektrokrakens, who depended on them for food, starved.

In 2010, a hungry elektrokraken swam south. The monster attacked a fishing boat in the North Sea, killing dozens. Only Captain Abraham Peters survived the creature's onslaught. British marine ecologist Victoria Metherham interviewed him the next day.

"He was blathering on about a giant squid that electrocuted his crew," she says. "I could smell the whiskey on his breath. He told me he'd never drunk a day in his life—until the attack."

When the giant squid attacked her research boat, she couldn't deny the elektrokraken's existence. Not only was it real, it was heading straight for London's River Thames. It wouldn't find any whales there, but it would find the next best thing: dozens of lean athletes competing in the World Rowing Championships. Government authorities dismissed her warnings. "They thought I was as nuts as Ahab," she says.

Nuts or not, someone had to stop the elektrokraken before it reached the Thames. Metherham joined forces with Captain Peters, who was looking for revenge against the creature. Without a boat to call their own, they commandeered the French crew's rowboat at the World Rowing Championships. Metherham and Peters tracked the elektrokraken's movements by measuring the faint electrical impulses it generated when swimming. After luring it close to the rowboat with chum, they shot it with a harpoon wired to a portable generator. The generator's charge overloaded the elektrokraken's electrical cells, killing it at once. And in case you're interested, the French rowboat team forfeited their race.

Herman Melville's *Moby-Dick* (Excerpt)

Stories of giant squid have long enthralled readers. In this excerpt from an early draft of *Moby-Dick*, Herman Melville describes a fictional encounter with the creature we now call the elektrokraken.

Lo! a beast rose to the water's surface beside our boat. Almost forgetting for the moment all thoughts of Moby Dick, we now gazed at the most wondrous phenomenon that the secret seas have hitherto revealed to mankind. A vast pulpy mass lay floating in the water, innumerable long arms radiating from its center, curling and twisting like a nest of anacondas, as if blindly to catch at any hapless object within reach. It eyed us suspiciously before disappearing back into the murky depths with a brilliant blue flash of light.

Starbuck, still gazing at the agitated waters where it had sunk, with a wild voice exclaimed, "Almost rather had I seen Moby Dick and fought him, than to have seen thee, thou electric ghost!"

"What was that monstrosity?" said I.

"The great electric kraken. They say few whale-ships ever beheld its blue light and returned to their ports to tell of it."

But Ahab appeared unimpressed. "We are on a mission. We do not have time to be distracted by calamari," said the captain, heading below deck. "If that damned squid shows its face again, call me, Ishmael, for I shall take it out with my own fists."

AVOID ■ ■ ■ AVOID BECOMING ELEKTROKRAKEN prey by following this simple advice:

- **Think twice about becoming a commercial fisherman.** Long hours that never seem to end. Difficult, back-breaking work.

CRAZY CONSPIRACY

One of the deadliest maritime disasters occurred on April 15, 1912, when the RMS *Titanic* sank into the North Atlantic Ocean. Trouble began the day before, when a lookout spotted an iceberg in the ship's path at 11:40 p.m. Despite attempts to maneuver around the obstacle, *Titanic* collided with the iceberg. Or so historians believe. Conspiracy theorists aren't so sure. How difficult is it to drive around a chunk of ice? The ship was attacked by an elektrokraken, they say. Some even wonder if the creature was drawn to *Titanic* by some mystical force, like that diamond Kate Winslet wears in the movie. Even if it didn't happen in real life, that would have been a much better film.

Terrible weather. Everyone knows the fishing life is rough. Throw in elektrokraken attacks, and it's just plain suicidal.

- **If you do go fishing, wear Crocs.** When an elektrokraken shocks your boat with an electrical charge, don't be caught off guard. Insulate your feet. Rubbery, waterproof Crocs work well. The other fishermen may laugh at your choice of footwear. They won't be laughing when they're dead.

SURVIVE ■ ■ ■ NO MATTER THE precautionary measures you take, you may still encounter an elektrokraken. Wearing your Crocs? Good. That's just the first step (no pun intended).

DON'T: Fall overboard. When an elektrokraken is shaking your boat, grab hold of something solid and stationary. Make sure it's not metal, unless you're hoping to save on your electroshock therapy bill.

DO: Boat with friends. If you're sprayed in the face with the elektrokraken's hallucinatory ink, someone needs to talk you down before you try flying from the top of the mast.

DON'T: Take pictures of the elektrokraken. Every time a colossal squid washes ashore, photos of it make the rounds on the Internet. No matter how tempted you are, stash your camera phone. Survival is more important than page views or retweets.

DO: Chainsaw the monster's arms off. Fin suggested this one. While we don't exactly know why you would have a chainsaw on a boat, wear rubber gloves if you're going to attempt to carve up an elektrokraken.

GATOROID

GATOROID

N ALLIGATOR'S JAWS ARE EVEN MORE POWERFUL than a shark's. Pump it full of performance-enhancing drugs until it's as big as a Greyhound bus, and it could swallow a great white. Gatoroids are surprisingly quick and agile for their size. While they prefer the taste of their unnatural enemy, the mega python, they'll settle for overturning your car to get at the fresh meat inside.

STUDY ■ ■ ■ WHEN HUNTERS COULDN'T contain the Everglades' invasive Burmese python population in 2011, park ranger Terry O'Hara devised an ingenious plan. She would singlehandedly restore nature's balance.

"We need a bigger gator. The balance of nature must be preserved," herpetologist Diego Ortiz recalls the park ranger saying. "She introduced anabolic steroids and experimental growth hormones into the gators' food supply. You have to understand that she was incredibly distraught at the time. Her fiancé had been killed by one of the snakes. The entire ecosystem of the Everglades hung in the balance. She felt the pythons were coming for her, to take away everything she held dear."

Unexpectedly, the gators multiplied in size. Their bones were barely able to carry their oversized muscles. These "gatoroids" fought back against the pythons, temporarily evening the score. Eventually, O'Hara was forced to destroy the monsters she'd helped create (see **MEGA PYTHON** for the rest of the story).

AVOID ■ ■ ■ ALLIGATORS HAVE BEEN around millions of years longer than human beings. We're living with them, not the other way around. Thankfully, alligators are native to just two places on Earth: the United States and China. Unfortunately, a quarter of the world's population lives in those two countries.

- **Respect alligators.** They're at the top of the food chain. They keep local animal populations under check in the areas they patrol. As long as we stay out of their way, we shouldn't have any problems with them. Say it out loud: R-E-S-P-E-C-T A-L-L-I-G-A-T-O-R-S.
- **Don't disrupt Mother Nature's food chain.** Mankind has a long history of upsetting nature's way of doing things. Even trying to do the right thing can have unintended consequences. Don't re-

Choosing the Right Weapon

So you've decided to step your game up and play offense instead of defense. Whether you're battling gatoroids or piranhacondas, we applaud your moxie. Here's a quick rundown of some of the most popular tools of the trade for would-be heroes.

Dynamite

When it comes to fighting monsters, dynamite is the weapon du jour. It's extremely effective, as O'Hara proved when she used it to rid the Everglades of gatoroids. It's also incredibly dangerous. Dynamite grows unstable over time. An old stick is as liable to explode in your hand as it is to detonate in a gatoroid's mouth.

Firearms

There are as many different makes and models of guns as there are unnatural threats. Finding the right gun for the right monster can be tricky. Shotguns work well against arachnoquake spiders, while nothing short of a semiautomatic rifle will take down a redneck gator. Train with a variety of firearms to be on the safe side.

Harpoon Guns

Sometimes, the best weapon is simply whatever's closest. When you're on a boat, that would be a harpoon gun (either deck-mounted or handheld). Harpoon guns have proven effective against dinosharks and pteracudas.

Chainsaws

If it can cut through a tree, it can cut through a monster. Some decry chainsaws as impractical. "The average chainsaw weighs ten pounds, compared to a two-pound machete," undead scholar Max Brooks writes in *The Zombie Survival Guide.* "Why increase the chances of exhaustion?" Because chainsaws look and sound awesome. That's why.

lease invasive pythons into the Everglades. And whatever you do, don't feed HGH- and steroid-infused chickens to alligators.

WEIRD SCIENCE

Why don't athletes who "juice" grow to the size of buildings like the gatoroids do? Authorities believe that, in addition to HGH and anabolic steroids, O'Hara fed the gatoroids an as-yet-unknown drug. Tests administered on the gatoroids by the US Anti-Doping Agency showed traces of a growth hormone unlike anything else for sale on the black market. Authorities are still searching for the supplier. Sports pundits are already calling for asterisks in the record books. "We're living in the Gatoroid Era," *Sports Annotated* columnist Skippy Bane says.

SURVIVE ▪ ▪ ▪ IF A GATOROID wanders into your backyard, let it be. You can't hurt it with that little peashooter you call a rifle, and you'd be crazy to use dynamite so close to your own house (see the sidebar, "Choosing the Right Weapon"). What happens if you run into a gatoroid in the wild?

- **Use knowledge of a gatoroid's anatomy to your advantage.** Alligators can only see side to side. If you're in a car or on foot, back away from the beast in a straight line. If a mega python corpse blocks your path (as is so often the case), charge forward underneath the gatoroid's belly and pray that it doesn't have a full bladder.

- **Take cover indoors or under a large object.** Gatoroids are used to feasting on mega pythons. Humans are quite small by comparison. If a gatoroid has to exert too much energy looking for you, it will move on. How much work would you do for an M&M that dropped between your couch cushions?

From the Kitchen of Diego Ortiz
Fried Gatoroid

Why I Love This Recipe: As a world-renowned herpetologist, I've studied a lot of reptiles. Gatoroids are among the most unique. They're the deadliest and most destructive. They're also the best-tasting. It might have something to do with the performance-enhancing drugs saturating their muscles. Don't worry—they're far less toxic than your average factory-farmed chicken breast. As long as you fully cook gatoroid meat, the worst side effect you'll experience is a full stomach.

Ingredients: 2 lbs. boneless gatoroid meat (tail cuts preferred), 1 tbsp. salt, 1 tsp. ground black pepper, 2 cups all-purpose flour, 2 cups buttermilk, 2 cups hot sauce, cooking oil

1. Cut gatoroid meat into 1"–2" cubes and season with salt and pepper.
2. Combine gatoroid cubes and flour in a plastic bag and shake until coated. Set bag aside.
3. Mix buttermilk and hot sauce in a bowl and dip the gatoroid chunks.
4. Using the plastic bag again, recoat gatoroid chunks in flour.
5. Heat cooking oil in sauté pan over medium-high heat to 375°F.
6. Fry for 3–5 minutes or until golden brown. Flip and cook for an additional 2–4 minutes.
7. Drain on paper towels and let rest 5 minutes.
8. Serve w/ ranch dressing or your favorite dipping sauce. See you later, alligator!

GHOST SHARK

GHOST SHARK

VITALS

ALSO KNOWN AS: Poltershark
FIRST OBSERVED: Smallport, Florida (2013) • **EST. MAX. SPEED:**
N/A (Teleports) • **HIGH-RISK GROUPS:** Kids Wading in Creeks,
Kids Playing near Busted Fire Hydrants, Kids Doing Cannonballs
into Pools • **LOOK OUT FOR IT IN:** All Water • **THREAT
TO HUMANITY:** 💀💀💀 • **RISK OF ENCOUNTER:** 🌀🌀 •
FIN'S WTF FACTOR: ⚠️⚠️⚠️⚠️⚠️

HOST SHARKS CAN MATERIALIZE ANYWHERE
there's water, from your backyard pool to a car
wash. They can hurt you, but you can't hurt them.
Sounds unfair, doesn't it? Too bad. Ghost sharks
don't care what you think. They don't have func-
tioning digestive tracts, either, which means their appetites are insatiable. They keep killing until stopped. Theoretically, a single ghost
shark could wipe out more than just the small beachside community
that antagonized it. It could wipe out all of humanity.

STUDY ▪▪▪ IN THE SEVENTEENTH century, a plague tore through a Spanish American settlement near the site of present-day Smallport, Florida. The infected were rounded up, transported to a cave during low tide, and executed. Soon after the murders, the angry dead rose up and ravaged the town. According to a diary dating back to this time, "Anyone who dies in the cave violently will rise again."

Anyone . . . and anything, as Smallport residents discovered in 2013 when a fisherman hooked a massive great white. Normally, such a rare catch would be cause for celebration. However, the shark swallowed the amberjack already on the fisherman's line, costing him the $30,000 top prize in a fishing tournament. The fisherman and his daughter decided to cause the shark $30,000 worth of pain. They shot it in the face, poured hot sauce in its eyes, and dropped a live grenade into its mouth. The wounded shark floated into the aforementioned underwater cave and finally died . . . only to return in spirit form. Apparently, the curse was real. You can't make this stuff up. The ghost shark attacked its killers, rendering them a bloody mess.

Unfortunately for the sleepy resort town of Smallport, the ghost shark's quest for vengeance did not stop there. It sought revenge on the entire town. The angry spirit used water as a conduit to teleport around Smallport, devouring innocent men, women, and children.

"When my friends and I learned of the magical cave, we knew it had to be the key to stopping the ghost shark," says Ava Reid, a high-schooler wise beyond her years. With the help of local drunk and lighthouse aficionado Darnell Finch, the teen dynamited the cave, ending the ghost shark's reign of terror. "For a minute, I was in seventh heaven. Then it sank in that the ghost shark had killed most of my friends. It killed my father. Could the cave have somehow brought them back to life? Destroying the cave was a double-edged sword."

Ghost-Hunting Tips

If the ghost shark is linked to a talisman, you may need to hunt the creature as you would any other ghost. That's not going to be as simple as blowing up a cave. Ghost hunting is demanding work. Make things a little easier with these helpful tips.

- **Never hunt alone.** Carry walkie-talkies or cell phones in case you're split up.
- **Don't trespass on private property.** While a ghost shark can cut you in two, so can the buckshot from a nervous homeowner.
- **Wear comfortable shoes.** They will come in handy when chasing after (or, let's be honest, running from) a ghost shark.
- **Record the time and place of encounters.** Nine out of ten times, ghost sharks are just teleporting around at random. But you never know. You may be able to establish a pattern and predict where the ghost shark will strike next.
- **Don't smoke.** Cigarette smoke may be mistaken for poltergeist activity, especially in the dark. Keep the air clear.
- **Don't wear perfume or cologne.** Some ghost hunters have reported unusual smells emanating before paranormal manifestations, and perfume or cologne may mask these scents. However, you'll still want to wear underarm deodorant—ghost shark hunting is a damn sweaty business.

What happens once you've cornered a ghost shark? It all depends on the enchanted talisman you're carrying. Most talismans come with step-by-step instructions for banishing ghost sharks from the mortal realm. Granted, they're usually tougher to decipher than the instructions for putting together Ikea bookshelves, but you'll eventually figure them out. If you picked your talisman up secondhand, the instructions may be missing. Try throwing it at the ghost shark, maybe?

Source: G.H.O.S.T. (Ghost Hunters Ohio Search Team).

WEIRD SCIENCE

Despite the prevalence of human spirits walking around in this plane, ghost animals are rare. With the mass of animals slaughtered every day for the food supply, why aren't farms overrun with haunted hogs? Paranormal investigators are divided on the reasons more ghost animals aren't reported. One belief is that only "intelligent species" have souls, and that dimwitted animals such as chickens are inherently soulless. Delicious, but soulless. Others believe that animal spirits aren't capable of being trapped on Earth—the "all dogs go to heaven" theory.

AVOID ▪ ▪ ▪ IT'S ANYONE'S GUESS as to how many more mystical caves are out there. In the meantime, avoid all water, including:

- Lakes, rivers, and creeks
- Toilets, bath tubs, and sinks
- Drinking fountains
- Garden hoses and sprinklers
- Slip 'N Slides
- Pools (both in-ground and aboveground)
- Your pet's water bowl
- Bottled water

Replace all water in your life with alcohol. Ghost sharks won't materialize if you're washing your hair with Bud Light and brushing your teeth with vodka.

SURVIVE ▪ ▪ ▪ SURVIVORS OF GHOST shark attacks are about as rare as the creatures themselves. So what can you do?

1. **Go on the offensive.** Be the hero. Someone needs to stop the ghost shark. Why not you? And please don't suggest calling the Ghostbusters. They haven't answered the phone since 1989.

2. **Forget everything you know about hunting sharks.** Everyone knows how to hunt a great white. You toss chum overboard to attract the shark, cram a scuba tank between its jaws, and shoot the tank. Unfortunately, ghost sharks aren't so easily defeated. There's no way to blow up something that doesn't have a physical body.

3. **Destroy the ghost shark's enchanted cave.** We suggest finding a qualified demolition expert to handle this task.

NOTE: *If the ghost shark is tied to an enchanted talisman instead of a cave, DO NOT destroy the magical object. See the "Ghost-Hunting Tips" sidebar for assistance.*

PIRANHACONDA

PIRANHACONDA

ITH THE HEAD OF A PIRANHA AND THE body of an anaconda, the piranhaconda is part snake, part fish, and all killing machine. Piranhacondas measure over 150 feet long— five times the size of the largest green anaconda. While their mouths are large enough to swallow prey whole, they prefer to use their dagger-like teeth to tear victims into smaller pieces first. Piranhacondas may not be lightning-quick, but they don't have to be. They just have to be faster than their prey (i.e., you).

STUDY ▪ ▪ ▪ THE HAWAIIAN ISLAND of Kauai is a birdwatching paradise, featuring endangered species such as the Hawaiian gallinule and red-footed booby. However, birders aren't the only ones flocking to Kauai for its avian attractions. Snakes love to feed on birds. In 2012, University of Hawaii professor of herpetology Dr. Bud Lovegrove discovered a new hybrid species of snake in Kauai— the monstrous piranhaconda. "I found dozens of giant eggs in the jungle, and did what any man of science would do in my position—I snatched one and busted ass," he says.

The proud parents went on a rampage, killing two dozen people while looking for Dr. Lovegrove and the stolen egg. B-movie actress Kimmy Weston (*Hillbilly Hostage*) and director Milo Christ (*Head Chopper*) were among those killed. Dr. Lovegrove lost an ear to a piranhaconda before a stuntman from the Milo Christ production dynamited the snakes to oblivion.

Was the egg—lost in the melee—worth the bloodshed? "There are six billion *Homo sapiens* on the planet," Dr. Lovegrove says. "Biologically speaking, we're a cheap commodity. The egg was a priceless evolutionary specimen."

AVOID ▪ ▪ ▪ AFTER LOVEGROVE RECOVERED and examined the piranhaconda corpses, he discovered they were both male. This means a third piranhaconda is still out there somewhere. With no eggs to care for, it may have left the island to find a new mate. It could be in Asia, South America, or your backyard.

- **Don't wander off into the jungle alone.** Also, don't tell your friends you'll "be right back." That's just asking to be mauled ironically.
- **Thou shalt not steal.** Despite living in close proximity to human populations, the piranhaconda in Kauai did not attack anyone until one of its eggs was stolen. If you venture into a nest

of football-sized eggs on your next tropical expedition, leave them as you found them.

SURVIVE ▪▪▪ PIRANHACONDAS ARE NOTORIOUSLY well camouflaged. Stumble across one by accident? You're not dead—yet.

- **Stop what you're doing.** If the piranhaconda hasn't spotted you, freeze. Piranhacondas rely heavily on movement to find prey. Your ringing cell phone won't give away your position, but answering it might. We're sure your significant other will understand.
- **Play hide-and-seek.** Finding someplace to hide won't be easy. Piranhacondas excel at this old children's game. Your options for shelter will be limited in the jungle. If you can make it to a car or helicopter, great. Avoid jumping into a body of water—piranhacondas weren't dubbed "river demons" on a whim.
- **Toss a grenade or stick of lit dynamite into its mouth.** Firearms will not penetrate the piranhaconda's thick skin, so the most vulnerable location to attack is its mouth. Unfortunately, an open mouth usually indicates the creature is seconds away from chomping down on you—at which point it's too late. We suppose you could pretend to yawn, and see if the piranhaconda opens its mouth at a safe distance. Yawning is contagious, right?

WEIRD SCIENCE

Could a piranhaconda survive a trip across the Pacific Ocean? The answer—it's not a comforting one for anyone in Asia or on the west coast of the Americas—is yes. While piranhas are freshwater fish, piranhacondas have respiratory systems like anacondas and other snakes. In other words, they breathe air. If a human being can survive in the open water, a piranhaconda could do the same.

PTERACUDA

PTERACUDA

VITALS

ALSO KNOWN AS: Barradactyl
FIRST OBSERVED: Mexico (2011) • **EST. MAX. SPEED:** 300 mph
• **HIGH-RISK GROUPS:** Sharktopi, Tourists • **LOOK OUT FOR IT IN:** All Environments • **THREAT TO HUMANITY:** 💀💀 • **RISK OF ENCOUNTER:** ⚡⚡ • **FIN'S WTF FACTOR:** △△△△△

IOWEAPONS ENGINEERS MASHED UP PTERODAC-
tyl and barracuda DNA to create the hideous pteracuda. Its sleek, torpedo-shaped body makes it fast in
the water and in the air. Its large, batlike wings aren't
just for flight—the pteracuda can also use them to
create thunderclaps strong enough to knock you off your feet. It will
then use its long tail to whip you into submission before moving in
for the kill with its sharp talons.

STUDY ▪▪▪ FROM HORSES TO dragons, humanity has long been using animals in warfare. As genetic engineering progressed, it was only natural (or unnatural?) that governments would use it to gain a competitive advantage on the world stage. "Some of the previous bioweapons experiments have been disastrous. But so have all of my previous marriages," Dr. Rico Symes, creator of the pteracuda, was overheard saying. "You want to make it in this business, you have to take risks."

The risk did not pay off. The pteracuda broke free on a training run in Mexican waters, attacking boaters and beachgoers along the coast. To stop the creature, Dr. Symes programmed a sharktopus (see **SHARKTOPUS**) with a single directive: Seek and destroy the rogue pteracuda. Dr. Symes also had a backup plan: mercenary Kirk "Ham" Hammerstein.

As the pteracuda and sharktopus battled each other for supremacy of the seas, Hammerstein rigged a harpoon gun with an explosive charge. While the two genetic freaks were locked in combat, Ham fired the harpoon into the pteracuda's abdomen. The sharktopus dragged the pteracuda underwater, where the charge went off. The explosion rocked Ham's boat, and the water went red. While both creatures are presumed to have died in the clash, the sharktopus's body has never been recovered.

AVOID ▪▪▪ ALTHOUGH THE PTERACUDA can conceivably fly anywhere in the world, it prefers coastal areas where it can hunt on both land and in the water. As you've probably picked up on by now, beaches are dangerous monster magnets. Stay safe by following these tips.

- **Don't wear jewelry to the beach.** Flashy jewelry may look great when you're at the club. To a pteracuda flying overhead, however, your bling looks like fish scales. Leave your gold chains at home. As Mr. T would say, "I pity the fool."

- **Wear sunscreen.** While this won't help ward off a pteracuda per se, it is sensible advice nonetheless.
- **Don't needlessly draw attention to yourself.** If you're twerking on the beach, a circling pteracuda could mistake you for a wounded animal.

SURVIVE ■ ■ ■ WITH THEIR ABILITY to attack by sea, air, and land, pteracudas are Mother Nature's Navy SEALs. How can you defend yourself from an aerial and amphibious threat?

- **If it's dive-bombing you from the air, bury yourself in the sand.** It might lose sight of you. Also, no one likes to eat food covered in sand. No one.
- **Locate the closest volleyball net.** If a bunch of hardbodies are playing, snatch the ball from them and give it a good kick down the beach. As the players race after the volleyball, the pteracuda might chase them instead of you.

Monster Mashup

It seems like a day doesn't pass without some mad scientist creating a new creature by splicing existing ones together. Pteracuda. Sharktopus. Mermantula. What will tomorrow bring? We asked a panel of (sane) scientists to share their predictions with us.

- Wolverinah (Wolverine + Cheetah)
- Flying Sea Wasp (Jellyfish + Wasp)
- Snapping Taranturtle (Snapping Turtle + Tarantula)
- Rhinosaurus (Rhinoceros + *Tyrannosaurus rex*)
- Mangoose (Human + Mongoose)

REDNECK GATOR

REDNECK GATOR

EDNECK ALLIGATORS ARE A MUTANT SPECIES OF American alligator named for the deep crimson bands around their necks. While they might have a funny name, there's nothing humorous about these twelve- to fifteen-foot Cajun creatures. Even if they didn't have red necks, you could distinguish them from regular gators by the large, dischargeable quills at the ends of their tails. All it takes is one of these spikes through the gut to put a damper on your day.

STUDY ▪ ▪ ▪ WHEN PREDATOR PLANET producers received a tip in 2013 about a new species of gator, Tristan Sinclair, host of *The Gator Whisperer,* hopped on the first flight to the bayou to investigate. "Alligators are prehistoric relics as old as the dinosaurs," Sinclair wrote in his bestselling book *What Does the Gator Say?* "I've lived amongst the gators. I've unlocked their secrets."

The gators he found in the swamps of Vernon City, Louisiana, were unlike any he'd ever seen. "They were beautiful creatures. Beautiful ... and deadly," he says. While filming a segment for his show in a nest of redneck gator eggs, Sinclair and his crew were ambushed by a pack of angry gator parents. "It was a tragic day for gator-human relations," Sinclair says. "Not only did several hardworking *Gator Whisperer* crew members lose their lives, but I did something I'd never done before. I took a gator's life. It was in self-defense. That doesn't excuse it." The ordeal still haunts Sinclair. "Redneck or not, I pray every day for that gator," he says.

The sheriff's department issued a statement to the press that the redneck gator problem was "conclusively dealt with"—presumably meaning the species was wiped out.

AVOID ▪ ▪ ▪ IF YOU MUST go to the southeastern United States (or if you live there), follow these guidelines.

- **Keep away from open freshwater.** If you lose a golf ball in a pond, leave it be. Don't risk losing your life to a redneck gator lounging at the water's edge.
- **Carry a firearm or crossbow with you everywhere.** Live every day like you're in an apocalyptic wasteland. Respect all local ordinances (although in some places it's probably illegal *not* to carry a gun).
- **Don't sign up for one of those expensive redneck gator-hunting expeditions.** While the red-tinted skin can fetch a hefty

You Might Be a Redneck Gator If . . .

There are whispers in the bayou that even if you survive a redneck gator bite, you're still dead. Within twenty-four hours, the skin around the bite turns metallic green and scaly. Next, you lose control of your motor skills. Your body slowly breaks down at a cellular level. When the transformation is complete, you're no longer a redneck—you're a redneck gator. The transformation is irreversible.

If the stories are true, redneck gators may be the result of a virus—and not a mutation, as scientists currently believe. Autopsies performed on recovered redneck gator bodies have proven inconclusive. While this all sounds inconceivable, remember that less than fifty years ago we believed werewolves were fictional.

price on the black market, poaching redneck gators is illegal—and stupid. Many would-be poachers have been found faceup in the backwater, crossbow in one hand and a foot-long quill sticking out of their chest.

SURVIVE ▪ ▪ ▪ REDNECK GATORS ARE not natural aggressors, and they'll typically retreat—unless they feel threatened.

- **If you see a redneck gator, quietly back away.** Act like you're trying not to wake a baby. A baby that can eat you.
- **If you're attacked and have a weapon, aim for its red neck.** The red band is known as the "kill spot"—the redneck gator's most vulnerable external location. That doesn't mean that penetrating its hide is easy.

ROBOCROC

ROBOCROC

ALTWATER CROCODILES ARE AMONG THE LARGEST terrestrial predators in the world. A twenty-five-foot-long adult croc can crush a cow's skull between its jaws. A robocroc, on the other hand, can crush a car. Once it catches you between its steel jaws, it will whip you around with sudden jerks of its head. This process (known as "death rolling") is meant to tear you into manageable pieces. By the time it begins swallowing chunks of meat and bone, you're (hopefully) dead.

STUDY ■ ■ ■ WHILE A US Army spokesperson feigned ignorance regarding military involvement in the 2013 robocroc incident, a freedom-of-information request revealed the true extent of the experiment gone wrong. The documents, although heavily redacted, paint the picture of a disturbing weapon of mass destruction inadvertently set loose on US soil. The army's nanotech weapons system was originally designed for deployment behind enemy lines. While we don't know where the rocket carrying the nanobots was headed, we do know where it crashed: Tampa's Adventure Cove.

Once in the park, the nanobots latched onto Stella—a 2,300-pound saltwater crocodile. Within hours, the nanobots replicated throughout Stella's body, changing the animal from flesh and blood into a cybernetic organism—a robocroc.

The military had given the nanobots a simple root-level directive: SURVIVE. The robocroc viewed anyone it crossed paths with as a potential threat, treating them accordingly. "I had to stand by and watch in horror as the animal I once knew as Stella began attacking water park visitors," zookeeper Jim Duffy says. "She should have been sated with just one meal. Maybe two, if she caught small children without much meat on their tiny bones."

WILD WARFARE

EMP weapons fry all electronics within range, including nanobots. Obviously, this is a weakness in the "nanobots are the wave of future warfare" argument. All an enemy would need is a few machines capable of generating electromagnetic pulses to neutralize an army of cyborg creatures—perhaps another reason the US shut down the controversial weapons program.

How to Apply a Tourniquet

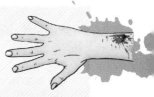

A robocroc just severed your friend's arm. Unless she gets medical attention, she's going to die. Luckily for her, you read this book. You are now the next best thing to a trained medical professional.

1. You will need something to tie around the limb, such as a rope or belt. If neither is available, a rolled-up T-shirt will work.
2. Tie the tourniquet around the limb, at least two inches above the wound. Do not apply to a joint. Tighten as much as possible. Your goal is to stop the blood flow completely.

WARNING: Tourniquets should only be applied to severed limbs. If the robocroc bit off your friend's entire lower body at the waist, don't waste your time (or your T-shirt) trying to tie a tourniquet around her abdomen.

Duffy finally stopped it with a non-nuclear electromagnetic pulse (EMP) weapon, frying the robocroc's circuitry. "By that point, Stella was more machine than animal," he says, his eyes filled with tears. "I did what had to be done."

AVOID ■ ■ ■ ARE THERE MORE robocrocs on the horizon? Or could nanobots latch onto a different host animal, such as a prehistoric cave bear? For the time being, probably not. The government's nano-tech program has officially been shut down. Engineers believe the program was one of a kind. Other countries and organizations are still years away from possessing similar technology. But make no

Crocodiles as Weapons of War

Robocrocs aren't the first time crocodiles have been drawn into mankind's war games. Saltwater crocodiles are blamed for the deaths of anywhere from four hundred to one thousand Japanese soldiers in the Battle of Ramree Island on February 19, 1945. British soldiers cornered a thousand Japanese soldiers in the swamps on the Burmese island of Ramree—which, unbeknownst to both sides, was home to scores of saltwater crocodiles. In the darkness, the crocs tore the Japanese to shreds. "At dawn the vultures arrived to clean up what the crocodiles had left," British soldier and naturalist Bruce Wright reported. While the exact number of dead is heavily disputed—some historians doubt the veracity of Wright's story, which has never been corroborated—the Battle of Ramree Island was listed in the *Guinness Book of World Records* as the record holder for "The Greatest Disaster Suffered from Animals." After nearly seventy years of dominance, the battle was displaced in the 2014 edition of the record book by the Los Angeles sharknados.

mistake—nanotechnology is here to stay. And it will be weaponized. Eventually, *everything* will be weaponized. You can't avoid the future. You can only survive it.

SURVIVE ▦ ▦ ▦ WHETHER A ROBOCROC attacks you or passes you by depends on its programming. Don't take chances—be ready.

- **Shoot at it—but don't expect results.** Tranquilizer darts, heavy artillery, and even grenades are useless against a robocroc's metal exoskeleton. Nerve gas and other biochemical weapons are also ineffective. If a robocroc charges you, fire at it with whatever weapon you're carrying. It will at least give you something to do in your final moments, distracting you from your life flashing before your eyes.

- **Deploy an EMP weapon.** Outside of a direct nuclear strike capable of melting the nanobots, a localized EMP weapon is your best chance to shut a robocroc down. The military probably has a stockpile. If they don't show up in time, check eBay. You can buy anything there. Someone once tried to sell stolen human brains on eBay. What kind of sick world do we live in? Don't answer that.

SHARKTOPUS

SHARKTOPUS

VITALS

ALSO KNOWN AS: S-11
FIRST OBSERVED: Puerto Vallarta, Mexico (2010) • **EST. MAX.**
SPEED: 35 mph • **HIGH-RISK GROUPS:** Bikini-clad Sunbathers,
Bikini-clad Bungee-jumpers, Bikini-clad Beach Yoga Practitioners •
LOOK OUT FOR IT IN: Saltwater • **THREAT TO HUMANITY:** 💀💀💀
• **RISK OF ENCOUNTER:** 🦑🦑 • **FIN'S WTF FACTOR:** ⚠⚠⚠⚠

LOOK OUT: THE SHARKTOPUS IS EIGHT-ARMED AND dangerous. With the head and partial body of a shark anchored by long octopus arms, this genetic aberration is the very definition of "unnatural." US government contractor Blue Water Corp designed the sharktopus to be the ultimate biological weapon. By transmitting focused electrical charges from a collar to receptors implanted within the creature's cerebral cortex, Blue Water thought they could control it. If you've seen video of the sharktopus online, you know this hybrid horror doesn't like to take orders. It likes to take lives.

STUDY ▪ ▪ ▪ THE SHARKTOPUS PROGRAM cost US taxpayers a whopping $456 million. Pentagon officials insist the potential upside was worthwhile. A single sharktopus, they argued, could replace entire platoons of Navy SEALs. It could sneak into hostile waters to hunt down pirates without being detected. "Just imagine how cool it would have been to send one of these things in to rescue Captain Phillips," an anonymous Pentagon official says.

On a training run in 2010, the sharktopus broke free of its control collar and started attacking tourists in Puerto Vallarta. Attempts to shut it down remotely failed. Blue Water CEO Nathan Sands, fearing his pet project would be killed, attempted to hire back ex-employee Andy Flynn to bring the sharktopus in alive. Flynn refused. The runaway weapon had to be destroyed, not taken alive. Too many lives had already been lost. "The civilian lives are a tragedy, but greatness comes at a price," Sands allegedly said before dying at the creature's tentacles.

While Flynn fought with the sharktopus, Nicole Sands—Nathan's daughter and co-creator of the creature—hacked the kill switch buried deep within its brain, terminating it. "When you mess with Mother Nature, she messes with you right back," Flynn says. "I don't even eat genetically modified foods now."

WEIRD SCIENCE

The sharktopus's rampage through Puerto Vallarta shocked biologists. "Sharks aren't serial killers. They kill for a purpose. And octopi are smart as hell. They wouldn't show themselves like that," Andy Flynn told the House Committee on Unnatural Affairs. As Congress would later learn, Blue Water enhanced the creature's aggressiveness by disrupting the serotonin levels in its brain. When they released it into open water for its big test, it was blind with rage. All it could do was bite down and tear things apart.

How to Tie Sharktopus Tentacles into a Knot

Let's say you're on a group dive when a sharktopus attacks. You have no weapons underwater. You have no way to call for help. You only have your hands. Thankfully, that may be all you need to fight back.

1. While another member of your group distracts the sharktopus, swim up behind it.
2. Grab two sharktopus tentacles about three feet from the ends. Avoid touching the suction cups, which are difficult to disentangle yourself from.
3. There are hundreds of knots at your disposal, such as the double fisherman's knot and the triple-nosed Portuguese sailor's slipknot. Even if you weren't in the Boy Scouts, you probably know a few different knots from *Fifty Shades of Grey*. It doesn't matter which knot you go with, so long as you can perform it quickly and accurately. Choose one, and tie the arms together securely.
4. Repeat three times, or until the sharktopus has stopped mauling your friend and turned its attention toward you.
5. Swim to the surface. With its arms tied, the sharktopus will be unable to leap out of the water after you.

AVOID ▪ ▪ ▪ ALTHOUGH BLUE WATER was shut down, the sharktopus threat is just beginning.

- **Not visiting Mexico anytime soon? Don't worry—the sharktopus will come to you.** An unknown number of fertilized eggs found their way into the wild. Full-grown sharktopi have already begun popping up around the world (see **PTERACUDA**).
- **Pay attention to sharktopus warning signs at beaches.** If there's been a recent sighting or attack, authorities will post tem-

porary notices warning beachgoers to stay out of the water for a specified period. If the sharktopus lingers, a permanent sign may be installed. Just because the beach is open, don't assume it's safe to go swimming or surfing. Politicians are lax to close recreation areas because of pressure from local businesses. And, for what it's worth, sharktopi are decidedly unique tourist attractions.

SURVIVE ▪ ▪ ▪ WITH ITS LONG arms, a sharktopus can reach you from at least thirty feet away. You're not safe anywhere on the water—or near it. Boats, jet skis, low-flying helicopters, airplanes, and hang gliders are all dangerous.

- **When a sharktopus leaps out of the water and begins stalking toward you, you better move it.** And we don't mean your booty. Time is of the essence. If you can get far enough inland, it

Naming the Sharktopus

While Blue Water Corp referred to their creation as "S-11," it soon gained another name thanks to Mexican English-language radio DJ "Captain" Jack Manning. Here's a transcript of his now-infamous recording, as aired on PV Pirate Radio:

Attention all hands. This is your captain speaking. We're getting more reports of this half-shark, half-octopus creature that's terrorizing the coast. Please don't panic! There is a way we can stop this thing. Virgin sacrifices. Yes, the Mexican Fish and Game Commission assures me the only way to appease this "sharktopus" is to offer it a beautiful virgin, preferably eighteen to twenty-five years old. I wish there was another way, but this is our only hope.

Shortly after this missive, Manning was killed by the sharktopus. Ironically, he died a virgin.

may give up on you. Despite its genetic modifications, a sharktopus cannot survive out of the water for very long.

- **Call in professionals (the ones who created the damn creature).** If you find a piece of a sharktopus's shock collar, inspect it for manufacturer information. Copy down the serial number and call their tech support hotline. If you're lucky, the corporation will be able to remotely shut the sharktopus down. If you're unlucky, you'll be stuck listening to Michael McDonald hold music for two hours before being disconnected just as a customer service representative comes on the line.

SWAMP SHARK

SWAMP SHARK

WHILE THESE DEEP-SEA SHARKS ARE NA-tive to ocean trenches, they can survive in freshwater as well—including in swamps, which is how they picked up their nick-name. They're thirty feet long and built like tanks. Instead of the smooth skin associated with other sharks, swamp sharks are covered in tough scales. With three rows of jagged teeth and an appetite to match, a hunter or fisherman in a pair of camouflage waders doesn't stand a chance against one of these armored behemoths.

STUDY ▪ ▪ ▪ IN 2011, RESEARCHERS retrieved a probe from a deep trench in the Gulf of Mexico. When they reeled it onto their boat, they realized a strange shark had followed the probe up from the depths. The shark attacked at once. By the time the coast guard answered their distress call, there was little left of the boat—or the researchers. Days later, a commercial boat captured the deep-sea shark while fishing for tuna. Realizing this was no regular shark, the captain sold it to an exotic-animal dealer.

As the dealer was transporting the shark through Louisiana, it escaped a containment tanker and slipped into Atchafalaya Bay. Despite receiving reports of shark attacks, local law enforcement dragged their feet. It was an alligator, they said. Local restaurant owner Rachel Broussard saw the shark's fin. "I've never seen an alligator with a fin before," she says. Broussard resolved to take matters into her own hands—with a little help from her family.

"My brother Jason is an ex–football player. I figured he could handle a swamp shark. He once faced down the scariest creature alive: a New York Giants defensive lineman," she says.

The Broussards lured the swamp shark into shallow water. After they weakened it with a grenade blast, they shredded the shark in the spinning blades of a pontoon. Rachel was relieved, but also a little frustrated. "There wasn't even enough of the shark left over to mount on the wall," she says.

WEIRD SCIENCE

How long can a swamp shark survive in freshwater? We don't know for sure. Some saltwater fish—notably, bull sharks—have been known to live for weeks in freshwater. The swamp shark in Atchafalaya Bay didn't need weeks to terrorize the local population. All it needed was three bloody days.

Off the Deep End

Besides swamp sharks, what else is swimming around in deep-sea trenches? Aquatic expert Dr. Lonnie Vargas is here to enlighten us.

- **Animals with frightening names.** Scientists love to christen deep-sea creatures with the most frightening names imaginable. The vampire squid. The Pacific viperfish. The coffinfish. The sea cucumber.
- **Aliens.** "The bottom of the ocean is still like an alien world to us," Vargas says. "We've even found aliens down there—most recently, the Bermuda tentacle monster." A military envoy encountered this hulking creature in the Bermuda Triangle. Historians have tied it to the disappearance of hundreds of ships and aircraft over the years.
- **More sharks.** Mother Nature, third-graders, and cable executives agree—there is no such thing as too many sharks.

AVOID ▪ ▪ ▪ THE NEXT DEEP-SEA shark to surface could be even larger and more dreadful than the swamp shark. Will it find its way to a freshwater swamp? Or will it acquire a taste for saltwater beach-goers, like the thawed dinoshark? No one knows.

- **If you're gushing blood from an open wound, don't go swimming.** Much like vampires, swamp sharks can smell a drop of blood miles away. Also, if you have a cut that hasn't healed, see a doctor. That can't be good.
- **Stay out of the water at night.** Swamp sharks are most active in the evenings—also like vampires. However, scientists have assured us that swamp sharks are not vampires. At least not yet . . .

SURVIVE ▪ ▪ ▪ DESPITE TAKING PRECAUTIONS, you may still run into a swamp shark now and again. Don't despair! It's not time to hit the bottle and drown your sorrows just yet. That comes later.

DON'T: Play dead. You can't fool a swamp shark. It's on to your game.

DO: Get out of the water. You know the drill by now.

DON'T: Punch the swamp shark in the nose. While some advise this for fighting off other sharks, the swamp shark's exoskeleton is strong enough to withstand the intense pressure found at the bottom of the ocean. You'll break your hand if you punch its nose.

DO: Hit the swamp shark in its eyes and gills. The Three Stooges gave eye-poking a bad rap, but it's a legit offensive maneuver. A well-placed karate chop to the gills may also work. If you can break concrete with your hands, it's worth a try. If you have a weapon—say, a sharpened stake you were saving for a vampire hunt—use it on one of these vulnerable areas.

A FINAL NOTE TO READERS

No one should have to go through what my family went through. I wish I'd had a book like this when the storm started. Perhaps I wouldn't have decided to stay in my oceanfront, hillside home until the last minute. Although I'm talking about the sharknados, you could also say the same things about my divorce. The fact is, I didn't realize how dysfunctional our family had become until the sharknados.

Our son, Matt, was in flight school, without Fin's knowledge. Claudia was doing whatever it is she does. Art school or something. I'd moved on, and was seeing this guy from the Valley, Collin. Fin was off having a midlife crisis with his little bar in Santa Monica. He might have been dating his bartender, Nova. Actually, I think her name was Jenny-Lynn—Nova might have been her stripper name. Maybe she never hooked up with Fin. Maybe she saw that he would eventually break her heart.

That's all water under the bridge now. The lines of communication in our family are open again. We realized that our personal problems were nothing compared to what we faced that day. In some ways, the sharknados were a blessing in disguise. I realized how much we needed each other. If we hadn't set aside our petty arguments and worked together, our family would have been torn apart— for real. By sharks. There are no visitation rights in the afterlife.

I know it sounds like I'm romanticizing sharknados. That's the last thing I would ever do. Learn from our example, so that you don't have to repeat it. It shouldn't take an unnatural disaster for you to realize what's important. Hug your loved ones. Live each day to the fullest. Don't just survive—thrive.

—April Wexler
Los Angeles, CA
June 2014

APPENDICES

THE S.S.A.T.

(SHEPARD SURVIVAL ASSESSMENT TEST)

DO YOU HAVE the knowledge to survive Mother Nature, or are you destined to be another statistic? Test your skills now with the S.S.A.T.

You see a funnel. You:

A. Pull out your phone to tweet about it.
B. Wait until you know if it's filled with sharks before deciding if you'll take shelter in your basement or evacuate your home.
C. Grab your chainsaw and pop a few ibuprofen, because it's going to be a long day.

You find a nest of mega python eggs. You:

A. Kick them like soccer balls.
B. Leave them alone, because it's best not to disturb nature.
C. Pull that dynamite out of your backpack—it's finally time to put it to use.

Mongolian death worms have been sighted in Las Vegas. You:

A. Sit tight at the poker table, because you're on a hot streak.
B. Get out of town, because what happens in Vegas stays in Vegas.
C. Follow the worms' trail, because they're probably guarding treasure bigger than anything you'll win at the slots.

Authorities have declared a state of emergency due to the extreme-weather vortex above your city. You're out golfing with a friend. There's not a cloud in the sky. You:

A. Keep golfing until you see lightning or ice twisters. You paid for nine holes, and you're going to play nine holes, dammit.
B. Drop your clubs and run to the clubhouse, leaving the golf cart and your friend behind.
C. Tackle your friend to the ground and army crawl to the nearest water hazard.

You're swimming at the beach when your friend sees the tell-tale fin of a dinoshark. You:

A. Tell your friend that, technically, the "dinoshark" is not a shark but instead a prehistoric sea reptile known as a pliosaur.

B. Get out of the water.

C. Return to the beach. Pick up your harpoon gun, kiss your significant other who is sunbathing, steal a jet ski, and chase after the dinoshark.

A giant meteorite struck Earth two days ago. The sun is setting an hour later than it should, because the planet is out of alignment. You:

A. Say, "Awesome! Extra hour of daylight!"

B. Stop using electronics in anticipation of electromagnetic storms.

C. Call the White House and tell them to get the president on the line, because you've got a plan to stop the polar storm in its tracks.

Your friend confides in you that a redneck gator just bit him, but he somehow survived the attack. You:

A. Gawk at his wound and say, "Cool story, bro!"

B. Drive him to see a physician, even if he gets blood all over the back of your pickup bed.

C. Chop his head off with an axe before he turns into a weregator, because that's what friends are for.

There's a knock at your door. Two formally dressed young men tell you they're from the New Dawn doomsday cult. They hand you a flyer about the upcoming Stonehenge Apocalypse. You:

A. Give a polite but firm "no thanks" and close the door.

B. Take the flyer and say you need to discuss it with your spouse, even though you have no spouse. Report the cult members to the authorities.

C. Invite them in for tea, knock them out and tie them up, and interrogate them about their doomsday plans.

A pack of hungry cyboars has you surrounded in the midst of a boaricane. You:

A. Roll into a ball and hope the floodwaters carry you away.
B. Take your shirt off and wave it like a matador's cape in an effort to distract the cyboars.
C. Identify the leader of the pack and charge her, even if you don't have any weapons. Your hands are the only weapons you need.

A firenado just set your house ablaze. You:

A. Frantically run through the house, gathering all of your video game consoles. Yes, even the 8-bit one packed away in your basement. That's a collector's item now.
B. Run outside and dive into your backyard swimming pool to escape the firenado.
C. Round up as many fire extinguishers as you can find and tie them to a bicycle. Ride the bike into the firenado, praying it will extinguish the flames before your face melts off.

SCORING GUIDE

For every "a," give yourself 1 point.
For every "b," give yourself 2 points.
For every "c," give yourself 3 points.

TALLY YOUR SCORE.

Chum (10–17): You survived . . . this quiz. Unfortunately, you aren't going to last long in the event of an unnatural disaster. Don't fret! Reread this book and retake the quiz.
Survivor (18–25): Congratulations! You are a survivor. After Mother Nature does her worst, you'll be one of the few left standing.
Hero (26–30): You are more than a survivor. You are a hero. When duty calls, you answer. *Hello, Duty. I've been expecting your call. Of course I'm ready.*

UNNATURAL DISASTER KIT

YOU SHOULD ASSEMBLE and maintain a portable unnatural disaster kit that you can use at home or take with you if you must evacuate. Store the items in sturdy, clearly labeled, easy-to-carry containers. Duffel bags, backpacks, and covered trash receptacles are good candidates. Keep them by your front door. Don't let your husband throw them out with the trash.

Tools and Supplies
- Portable, battery-operated radio
- Flashlight and extra batteries
- First aid kit
- Cash, coins, and Chuck E. Cheese tokens
- Copies of personal identification, such as driver's licenses, passports, insurance cards, and credit cards
- An extra set of car keys and house keys
- Medications—prescription and nonprescription
- Kitchen accessories—can opener, disposable cups, plates, and other utensils
- Soap, shampoo, and other personal hygiene items
- Liquid bleach
- Acoustic guitar or ukulele
- Matches in a waterproof container
- Fire extinguisher (in case you start a fire with those matches)
- Clothing
- Scrapbook, scissors, and paste
- Blankets and sleeping bags—for Star Wars fans, ThinkGeek sells a nifty Tauntaun sleeping bag built for the wastelands of Hoth

Food and Beverages (three-day supply minimum)

- Water for drinking and cooking—one gallon per person/day
- Canned, nonperishable meats, fruits, vegetables, etc.—examples include fully cooked and canned Tactical Bacon™, jellied loaf of cranberry sauce
- Seasoning—salt, pepper, and hot sauce
- Packaged snacks—although not very nutritious, most processed foods like crackers and snack cakes have shelf lives longer than basilisks
- Don't forget your little ones—baby food and pet food
- Coffee, tea, and other caffeinated beverages—without caffeine, what's the point of surviving an unnatural disaster?

In addition to the three-day supply of food and water in your unnatural disaster kit, you should consider maintaining a two-week supply in your home. In your fallout shelter, keep a thirty-day supply. Under your bathroom sink, keep a couple of extra rolls of toilet paper. Not in case of an unnatural disaster, but just as a general guideline.

SOURCE: Adapted from *Talking About Disaster: Guide for Standard Messages.* Produced by the National Disaster Education Coalition, Washington, DC.

EMERGENCY SUPPLIES FOR YOUR VEHICLE

YOUR VEHICLE SHOULD be stocked with emergency supplies separately from your unnatural disaster kit.

- Properly inflated spare tire, wrench, and car jack
- Jumper cables
- Tool kit
- Flashlight and extra batteries
- Reflective triangle (a square would work too)
- Signal flares
- Ammunition for the most common firearms (including Nerf ammo for the kids)
- First aid kit
- Duct tape
- Grappling hook and rope
- Shovel, windshield scraper, and snowbrush
- Sand
- Tire chains
- Warm clothing
- Sleeping bag and blankets
- Tent
- Compass
- Life-size cardboard standee of Brad Pitt from *World War Z* (for inspiration)

Several of these supplies may appear useless at first glance. Why do you need warm clothing or tire chains if you live in Los Angeles? You should know by now that unnatural disasters do not obey traditional weather patterns. Prepare for ice twisters as well as sharkna-dos.

Additionally, many supplies have multiple uses that won't be-come obvious until the heat of the moment. While a grappling hook could be used to scale a cliff, it could also be used to lower you off a bridge to save a bus full of children. Even if you never need to use it, it will still make you feel like a super-sweet ninja. Confidence is vitally important during emergencies.

SOURCE: Adapted from *Talking About Disaster: Guide for Standard Messages.* Produced by the National Disaster Education Coalition, Washington, DC.

Space Sharknado
by Charlie Price (Excerpt)

CHARLIE PRICE IS the bestselling author of *Ionos-fear, Twisted Ice,* and two dozen other thrillers. He's a former scientist who traded fact for fiction—although he occasionally steps out of retirement when the fate of the world is on the line (see **ICE TWISTER**). Here is an exclusive excerpt from his forthcoming book *Space Sharknado.*

◦◦◦

SANDY TOOK A deep breath. She held it inside for what felt like an eternity. She couldn't let go, she couldn't let go, she couldn't— She exhaled. It was the last deep breath she would be taking for a while. Possibly forever. Her oxygen supply was limited to six more hours at most. Her ride home—the space shuttle *Exogenesis*—floated by her in pieces.

She'd been on a routine spacewalk when trouble started. While she was repairing a damaged section of the hull, a meteor shower struck. Hundreds of rocks—some as small as golf balls, others the size of her helmet—punched through the shuttle. Miraculously, Sandy escaped injury. Just a few small nicks in her space suit. No rips. The repairs to the shuttle she'd been about to make on the spacewalk were the least of her worries—because there was no shuttle anymore. Just debris.

Debris . . . and sharks.

Dozens of them. Hammerheads. Tiger sharks. Great whites. All let loose from the *Exogenesis*'s cargo bay. If they'd been ordinary sharks, they would have died in the vacuum of space. But these weren't ordinary sharks. They'd been created in a lab. Instead of respiratory systems that extracted oxygen from water, the sharks had photosensitive cells throughout their bodies for converting solar radiation into energy. At least that was how she understood it. For the scientific explanation, you'd have to ask their creator—some megalomaniacal genius, she guessed. Sandy was just an astronaut transporting them to the space station for live testing. They were too dangerous to let loose on Earth. Now they were floating all around her. The closest she'd come to one was fifty feet. It hadn't seen her. At least her bosses would know the experimental creatures could survive in space like they'd theorized. One small step for mankind. One great leap for sharks.

She could see the space station a mile away. If she could reach it, she could dock and forget this whole mess. Unfortunately, that would never happen. As Sandy orbited the Earth toward the station, the station drifted in its own orbit. Instead of getting closer, it was getting farther out of reach.

Something brushed against her leg. She glanced down just in time to see an enormous great white passing by. Ignoring her. It moved fast, and soon it was a speck in the distance. That was a close call. Too close. Suddenly, the great white appeared to grow larger. Was it . . . doubling back around? Impossible! There was no way a shark could navigate in space. Not even a genetically modified shark. It went against every scientific principle she knew.

But her eyes weren't lying.

The creature had somehow reversed course.

It swam past her again, at arm's length this time. Close enough to see its eyes were blacker than space. It had been testing her earlier to see if she was edible. Now it was circling her. Soon, it would move in for the kill.

Surviving the meteor storm wasn't a miracle; it was a curse. She wouldn't need to stretch out her oxygen after all. She closed her eyes and drew another deep breath. "Don't give up hope," she told herself. "There's always hope."

A lie. Hope was just another four-letter word.

Sandy exhaled, long and slow. She opened her eyes. That's when she saw it. Her savior, floating within arm's reach.

The chainsaw.

A Whale of a Bad Time: A Story of Survival

by Wilma Summers (Excerpt)

WILMA SUMMERS AND her husband Doug were on the disastrous 2008 Regal Islands International cruise that caused the Glacier Bay whalestrom (see **WHALESTROM**). In this excerpt from her 2012 memoir, Summers describes the hellish conditions the passengers endured.

⚮

BEFORE WE BOUGHT our tickets, I read a review of the *Regal Jewel* where this woman called it a "prison ship." I laughed. Though we'd never traveled with Regal Islands, Doug and I were veterans of the cruise scene. We'd been cruising for almost thirty years. In my experience, there are two types of people in this world: those who love to cruise, and those who love to complain when any little thing goes wrong. I think our granddaughter calls them "haters."

Flash-forward six months to our vacation aboard the alleged "prison ship," the *Regal Jewel*. Imagine our surprise when we learned the reviewer wasn't exaggerating!

Our ocean-facing room's porthole gave us an excellent view . . . of the lifeboats. The only time we could actually see the water from our "ocean view" room was during the whalestrom, after the crew lowered the lifeboats into the water.

The buffet was lousy. By the second day of the cruise, people were getting sick all over the place. I think it was the coconut shrimp. I didn't have any, but poor Doug! He threw up over the railing and onto one of the lower balconies. Then people on that balcony threw up onto the one below, and so on for seven levels. It was just awful. It's a miracle anyone even lived long enough to be killed by the whales.

After the ship began sinking, packs of children started running through the hallways at all hours of the night. Who was watching them? No one. It was like *Lord of the Flies*. I swear I saw a kid walking around with a pig head on a stick! Where were their parents? Some were dead, but surely not all of them.

And don't get me started on the evening entertainment. I'm sorry, but isn't "entertainment" supposed to be "entertaining"? One comedian ended his act with a ten-minute whoopee cushion routine. To my ever-loving horror, people actually laughed at this. The only time I laughed at him was when he fell overboard, and that was just because of the way he was swinging his arms. You probably had to be there.

FILMOGRAPHY

HOLLYWOOD HAS DRAMATIZED many of the unnatural threats documented in this book. Here is a partial list of movies, originally broadcast on Syfy. Most are now available on Blu-ray, DVD, and digital download/streaming. Thank you to Thomas Vitale, Chris Regina, and the Syfy Original Movies team for sharing these stories of mayhem and bravery—so that we, too, might learn how to become everyday heroes.

Arachnoquake. Dir. Griff Furst. Syfy Pictures/Active Entertainment, 2012.

Basilisk: The Serpent King. Dir. Stephen Furst. Syfy Pictures, 2006.

Bigfoot. Dir. Bruce Davison. Syfy Pictures/The Asylum, 2012.

Dinoshark. Dir. Kevin O'Neill. Syfy Pictures/New Horizons Picture, 2010.

Ghost Shark. Dir. Griff Furst. Syfy Pictures/Active Entertainment, 2013.

Ice Twisters. Dir. Steven R. Monroe. Syfy Pictures/Cinetel Films/Ice Twisters Productions/Insight Film Studios, 2009.

Manticore. Dir. Tripp Reed. Syfy Pictures/Unified Film Organization/Secure Productions, 2005.

Mega Python vs. Gatoroid. Dir. Mary Lambert. Syfy Pictures/The Asylum, 2011.

Meteor Storm. Dir. Tibor Takács. Syfy Pictures/Unity Pictures, 2010.

Mongolian Death Worm. Dir. Steven R. Monroe. Syfy Pictures/Black Chrome Productions/Sweet Tater, 2010.

NYC: Tornado Terror. Dir. Tibor Takács. Syfy Pictures/Fast Productions Ltd./Fast (Tornado) Productions, 2008.

Piranhaconda. Dir. Jim Wynorski. Syfy Pictures/New Horizons Picture, 2012.

Polar Storm. Dir. Paul Ziller. Syfy Pictures/Cinetel Films/Insight Film Studios, 2009.

Ragin' Cajun Redneck Gators. Dir. Griff Furst. Syfy Pictures/Active Entertainment, 2013.

Robocroc. Dir. Arthur Sinclair. Syfy Pictures/UFO International, 2013.

Rock Monster. Dir. Declan O'Brien. Syfy Pictures/RM Productions, 2008.

Sharknado. Dir. Anthony C. Ferrante. Syfy Pictures/The Asylum/Southward Films, 2013.

Sharktopus. Dir. Declan O'Brien. Syfy Pictures/New Horizons Picture, 2010.

Sharktopus vs. Pteracuda. Dir. Kevin O'Neill. Syfy Pictures/New Horizons Picture, 2014.

Stonados. Dir. Jason Bourque. Syfy Pictures/Two 4 The Money Media, 2013.

Stonehenge Apocalypse. Dir. Paul Ziller. Syfy Pictures/Cinetel Films/Reel One Pictures/Movie Central Network/The Movie Network/Super Ecran/SA Films, 2010.

Swamp Shark. Dir. Griff Furst. Syfy Pictures/Bullet Films, 2011.

Swamp Volcano. Dir. Todor Chapkanov. Syfy Pictures/Bullet Films, 2011.

ABOUT THE AUTHOR

ANDREW SHAFFER is a humorist and author whose works include *Literary Rogues, Great Philosophers Who Failed at Love,* and *Fifty Shames of Earl Grey.* He has appeared as a guest on FOX News, CBS, and NPR, and has been published in *Mental Floss, Maxim,* and *The Daily Beast,* among others. You can find him online at www .andrewshaffer.com.

FINLEY "FIN" SHEPARD is a former champion surfer. He lives in Los Angeles, and loves both of his children equally.

APRIL WEXLER is a sharknado survivor.